Is Wildness Over?

Environmental Futures

Will Big Business Destroy Our Planet?
Peter Dauvergne

Will China Save the Planet? Barbara Finamore

Is Wildness Over? Paul Wapner

Paul Wapner

Is Wildness Over?

polity

The right of Paul Wapner to be identified as Author of this Work has been asserted in accordance with the UK Copyright, Designs and Patents Act 1988.

First published in 2020 by Polity Press

Polity Press
65 Bridge Street
Cambridge CB2 1UR, UK

Polity Press
101 Station Landing
Suite 300
Medford, MA 02155, USA

ISBN-13: 978-1-5095-3211-7
ISBN-13: 978-1-5095-3212-4 (pb)

A catalogue record for this book is available from the British Library.

Library of Congress Cataloging-in-Publication Data

Names: Wapner, Paul Kevin, author.
Title: Is wildness over? / Paul Wapner.
Description: Cambridge ; Medford, MA : Polity, 2020. | Series:
  Environmental futures | Includes bibliographical references.
Identifiers: LCCN 2019035362 (print) | LCCN 2019035363 (ebook) | ISBN
  9781509532117 (hardback) | ISBN 9781509532124 (paperback) | ISBN
  9781509532148 (epub)
Subjects: LCSH: Naturalness (Environmental sciences) | Nature
  conservation--Philosophy. | Environmentalism--Philosophy.
Classification: LCC GE40 .W366 2020 (print) | LCC GE40 (ebook) | DDC
  304.2--dc23
LC record available at https://lccn.loc.gov/2019035362
LC ebook record available at https://lccn.loc.gov/2019035363

Typeset in 11 on 15 pt Sabon by
Servis Filmsetting Ltd, Stockport, Cheshire
Printed and bound in Great Britain by TJ International Limited

To Diane

For honoring my wild aspirations and forgiving
my too civilized neuroses

Contents

Acknowledgments

This is a thin volume, yet my debt in writing it extends far and wide. I wish to thank Louise Knight of Polity for inviting me to write the book and for her insightful editorial support. I am grateful to Nasruddin Chowdhury, Jessie Mehrhoff, Aimee Seligman, and Bryan Hickel for superb research assistance. Two anonymous reviewers offered incisive, challenging, and productive criticism; the book is far better for their efforts. A summer grant from the School of International Service at American University provided much appreciated research support and my students in the Global Environmental Politics Program consistently challenged me to write with greater purpose. Conversations with the Takoma Park Poetic Skull Sippers and the landscape of Taos, New Mexico served as ideal venues for exploring wildness. A special thanks goes to the

Acknowledgments

Lama Foundation, Association for Contemplative Mind in Higher Education, and EarthLoveGo.org for creating opportunities to share insights from this book. I would also like to acknowledge Richard Falk, my long-term mentor and friend, who has shaped my thoughts in ways beyond expression. Many other dear friends have enriched my life while I was researching and writing the book. I thank them for sharing their warmth and being themselves. My deepest gratitude goes to my family. Mindful of and engaged with the immense challenges facing our world, they demonstrate the amazing power of love.

1

Brave New Wild

Aldo Leopold, begins his classic environmental text *A Sand County Almanac* by distinguishing two kinds of people. He writes: "There are some who can live without wild things, and some who cannot" (Leopold, 1989, p. vii). He associates himself with those who cannot. Leopold, who lived from 1887 until 1948, loved the way the world moves on its own. He reveled in watching sunsets, rainstorms, flying geese, and foxes scampering across fresh snow. Encountering wildness, for Leopold, made life worth living. Wildness stands as something beyond human control and comprehension. It excites the mind, exercises the body, and elevates the spirit. Leopold spent his life celebrating wild things and working to protect them.

Leopold was one of the most thoughtful and perceptive environmentalists—a pioneer and visionary of ecology and environmental ethics. His comment about wildness, however, is overly polite. For a person who desperately wanted others to embrace a "land ethic" and care about the Earth, he makes it seem like wildness is a mere preference. Some just happen to love wild things; others not. This leaves out how political power shapes one's attitude to wildness. Moreover, he overestimates how many people share his love of wildness. Most people, even during Leopold's time, hate wildness. They may like sunsets and a season's first snow, but they find insects, thunderstorms, remote areas, and predatory animals irritating and often threatening. These things have their own way about them and this "otherness" can frustrate best-laid plans and prove unnerving in its unpredictability. Far from delight, wildness annoys and threatens. For most people, it is not something to marvel at or be moved by but a source of discomfort, inconvenience, and vulnerability. Over the past few centuries people have gone to great lengths to shove it out of their lives. When Leopold declared his love of wildness, he was a rarity—and he remains one today. Most people couldn't care less about wild things. They see well-being in stability and certainty and resist discomfort. The consequence of this, as I will explain, is catastrophic.

For many people, wildness is what we experience when we go into the woods, ascend a mountain, or explore a desert. Wildness, from this perspective, refers to the unwieldy character of the more-than-human world. In the woods, things happen on their own—in a manner that is indifferent and often resistant to human design. As the word's etymology suggests, 'wild' things are self-willed. They operate according to their own unique dynamics. For Leopold and fellow conservationists, encountering things that refuse to move to a human beat is a rush; it enlivens life. For most others, however, it spells annoyance and peril.

Wildness goes beyond forests and streams. It also shows up in human affairs. The unpredictability of war, mind-boggling complexities of high technology, and chaotic character of large crowds, for instance, share the element of uncertainty, tempestuousness, and danger. Wildness, in this sense, has to do with the capriciousness of living in a world of others. It denotes the unexpected dynamics that emerge in society and take on a life of their own. It is a state of mind where one loses one's bearings or finds oneself unable to manage circumstances. Some may like the unpredictable dimensions of collective life, just as they like wildness in the woods; most, however, detest it and do what they can to avoid it.

These days, the enemies of wildness have finally triumphed. They have largely realized the dream of ridding their lives of wild things. One sees this most dramatically among the affluent. Today the wealthy live protected from the elements, in secure houses or apartments; they avoid inconveniences by traveling in insulated cars or planes; and they have control over their immediate world through an almost infinite number of appliances. (Including transit, the average American spends over 93% of their time indoors: Klepeis et al., 2001.) Most buy food in a grocery store, draw energy from a plug, drink sanitized water, and flush waste down a toilet or sink. They track weather on cell phones, locate themselves through GPS, and flip a switch to get warmer or turn darkness into light. Many reside in stable regimes ruled by law or possess enough power to be otherwise secure. The most privileged have driver's licenses, medical care, protection from theft, education, and Internet service. Indeed, vast numbers of people today possess extraordinary control over their surroundings and find life more secure and enjoyable in the absence of wildness. To be sure, they still have ups and downs and unpredictable things still happen to them. The havens they have created are not impermeable. But they experience inconvenience and risk in increasingly circumscribed ways. For all intents and purposes, they have locked wildness out of their houses, occupations, and daily affairs. They have sent wildness into hiding. For them, wildness is over.

Global Wildness

Or so it seems. Looking around, even the most affluent must admit that the world is far from stable. People may have carved out sanctuaries of security and comfort but, all around them, things are coming undone. Calving glaciers, intensified storms, mass extinction, and the threat of nuclear annihilation suggest that wildness is far from being over. If anything, it has merely taken on a new face. Today unpredictability, instead of inconveniencing people's everyday lives, plagues the Earth as a whole. After centuries of being beaten down, the feral has reemerged—only this time across the planet and on steroids. The world now faces *global* wildness. Global wildness has come about not as an accident in humanity's long battle with otherness but as a direct consequence of it. In a twist of cosmic irony, by gaining more control and creating more predictability in their day-to-day lives, people have not gotten rid of wildness but transported it up to the planetary level.

Consider climate change. Harnessing energy to heat and cool one's home is the epitome of immunizing oneself from fluctuating weather. Likewise, using cars to travel long distances and manufacturing concrete for buildings enable people to live largely free from environmental imperatives. The same can be said of using lights, refrigerating food, and all carbon-rich activities. They represent attempts to minimize wildness, to enhance ease and predictability, and otherwise to control the world. Such attempts include using fossil fuels to generate wealth and power and to control other people. The problem, of course, is that, in the aggregate, these efforts do not rid life of wildness but merely displace it to the globe. They alter the planet's carbon cycle and thus throw the climate out of whack. Now, while many people may no longer have to battle discomfort locally, they must do so at the global level. And, while some people may have won greater power by harnessing fossil fuels, they must contend with greater powerlessness in the face of climate change.

The same goes for biodiversity loss. For centuries, people have worked to tame and protect themselves from the more-than-human world. They have hunted, built houses, used insecticides, and bred farm animals to insulate themselves from and control other creatures. They have also destroyed habitat by expanding cities and releasing poisons into the environment. The result is that, today, very few of the affluent encounter animals of any kind or even landscapes not significantly designed by humans. This may have solved the wildness problem for some locally—by immunizing them from immediate threats or inconveniences—but it has created a global wildness problem. It has triggered a cascading trophic decline that appears impossible to stop. Whole species are disappearing at rates unseen for the past 65 million years, and almost every species on Earth is facing decline in numbers, habitat, or health. Biodiversity is plummeting and ripping the fabric of life into threads. Despite many efforts to protect against such unraveling, biological collapse continues largely out of human control.

Global wildness goes beyond climate change and biodiversity loss. In search of comfort and security, humans have inserted themselves so deeply into the world around them that *all* ecosystems and the planet's infrastructure itself are now supercharged with a human signature. People have figured out not only how to extract fossil fuels and kill off innumerable creatures, but how to redirect rivers, deplete stratospheric ozone, cut down forests, release nuclear isotopes, and manufacture concrete and plastics in inordinate amounts, so that the latter now choke the oceans and promise to last indefinitely. Geoscientists note this impact by calling the present geological era the Anthropocene—"the age of humans." This indicates that humans have become *the* dominant ecological force (and that human influence will be discernible in the Earth's crust millions of years from now). The Anthropocene also means that, in affecting the planet's organic infrastructure, humans have set in motion developments that they can neither fully foresee nor control. Indeed, humanity has introduced so much unpredictability and danger into global systems that it now faces what Aldous Huxley might call "brave new wildness."

Displacing wildness to the globe is more than a strictly ecological event. Nuclear weapons were developed, theoretically, to preserve the peace. They represented a bigger, more menacing type of weapon whose very existence would deter conflict. Since war is, arguably, the most foreboding expression of wildness—with law, order, and customary kindnesses significantly breaking down—trying to minimize or eradicate it represents the epitome of getting rid of wildness. Of course, states also developed nuclear weapons not simply to preserve the peace, but to accumulate power and lord military strength over other nations. This was, in their own judgment, a way to exert control over and diminish the wildness of geopolitical affairs. The problem, however, is that, no matter whether the aim is peace or control, there is no end to building a bigger, more lethal arsenal; and thus, in the midst of trying to outlaw violent conflict or gain an upper geopolitical hand, the United States and Russia have engaged in a decades-long arms race that has left both of them with a veneer of safety and control at home but has created greater uncertainty globally. The attraction of nuclear weapons has enticed at least nine other states to develop arsenals and created enough collective firepower to destroy the world many times over. This points, again, to the irony of trying to eliminate wildness. In the effort to create a haven of security—whether to protect one's own citizens or exert control over other nations—nuclear powers have transported fragility to the global level. They have discharged something they themselves cannot fully control. They have traded the feeling of local security for global endangerment.

One sees a similar dynamic in world trade. In an effort to minimize fluctuations of local economies, increase efficiency, and gain control through economic dominance, states and corporations have cultivated and tried to excel in an interlinked economy. Economic globalization seemingly enables production and distribution to avoid the vicissitudes of local weather, wage requirements, or material availability. It also allows companies to take advantage of economies of scale so they can better penetrate markets and establish financial stability. The problem is that, in trying to bring more constancy to the local level and greater corporate control, economic globalization has created global fragility. Today economic interdependence brings financial precariousness to everyone. Too big to fail, the world economy stands not only as a planetary system of economic wealth generation and coercion but as a behemoth of economic industry that is vulnerable to unforeseen dynamics of tightly bound economic interdependence. Countries have purchased local security and corporations have sought self-regarding control at the price of possible international economic recession and collapse. Economic globalization, like nuclear weapons, reveals the paradox of humanity's battle with wildness. In its persistent efforts to get rid of wildness in daily encounters, humanity thrusts it upward to the globe. The Earth itself is now wild. The planet is in spasm.

Wild Injustice

Brave new wildness consists of catapulting unpredictability not only "upward," to the planetary level, but also "outward," to the margins of collective life. As mentioned, the privileged have mostly enjoyed the fruits of pushing wildness out of immediate experience. They are the main beneficiaries (as well as drivers) of fossil fuel development, industrialized farming, and nuclear weapons. However, wildness is figuratively akin to energy—it cannot be created or destroyed—and thus must go somewhere. As it gets squeezed out of people's immediate lives, it not only moves vertically but simultaneously gets thrusted horizontally, upon those living downstream. Today most environmental harms, economic dislocations, military assaults, and public health crises afflict the most vulnerable. In this sense, people rarely solve environmental problems, financial woes, or other collective afflictions; they displace them. They transport them to the lives of others. Thus the poor and those who have least contributed to the buildup of carbon dioxide and other greenhouse gases stand, disproportionately, at the receiving end of climate change. Likewise, the poor, who have been left out of international monetary deals, find themselves most vulnerable to economic shifts. And, when countries embark on military action in search of security, it is usually the underprivileged who do most of the fighting and suffer most civilian casualties. Wildness thus moves from the epicenters of power to the hinterlands. People thrust it outward to other communities.

That the privileged enjoy predictability and luxury partly on the backs of others merely gives form to what it means to move wildness to the global level. The global level is not a material platform on which wildness lands. Rather it is a complex socioecological network that involves over 7.7 billion people and countless living organisms and ecosystems. Wildness disseminates through these lineaments. This is why, as the world unravels in the face of increasing wildness, it does so, at first, along lines of social advantage. Historical stratification ensures that the least powerful bear the brunt. They have always been low on the totem pole of victimization. But, importantly, the unraveling does not stop there. Eventually global wildness spills over lines of privilege and establishes new routes of effect; eventually, through what sociologist Ulrich Beck (1992, p. 23) calls "the boomerang effect," it ensnarls even the wealthy and powerful. This is where horizontal and vertical displacement meet. Climate change, loss of biological diversity, and so forth register first on the bodies and nerves of the most vulnerable (Nixon 2011), but then go on to rattle and render fragile planetary systems. The poor and the politically weak may be on the frontlines of brave new wildness, but the frontier is increasingly receding. This does not mean that the privileged no longer enjoy tremendous protection from the vicissitudes of life; and it certainly does not mean that, since wildness has gone global, everyone is equally responsible for its displacement. It merely indicates that those who have successfully pushed wildness out of their lives are increasingly being swept up in the swirling globalization of unpredictability and lack of control. Wealth and political power are no longer sufficient insulating factors. The feral now haunts everyone.

Into the Wild

This book is about the fate of wildness. It describes the deep impulse to expunge risk, unpredictability, and inconvenience and how this has unleashed huge, unstoppable global challenges. At its core, the book illuminates a paradox. It shows how, in the effort to stamp out wildness, humanity has done the opposite: it has exacerbated rather than diminished the wild quality of life. The book explains, in other words, how the eradication of wildness from people's individual lives leads to global spasm.

The book goes further, however. It also wrestles with the question of what is to be done. Today various technologists are claiming that they know how to deal with global wildness. As they see it, the world can confront climate change, biodiversity loss, and other calamities by harnessing humanity's antipathy toward wildness and directing it at the globe itself. In other words, they want to fight global wildness with the same attitude, intelligence, and engineering power that have been used to push wildness out of people's individual lives—only this time with more muscle and on a larger scale. If the globe is going wild, constrain it; if the planet is in paroxysm, take control over it. For instance, as I will explain, geoengineers want of confront climate change by disciplining the atmosphere itself. They propose injecting chemicals into the sky to block sunlight or pulling carbon from the air to reduce the greenhouse effect. They see these as natural extensions of humanity's long-standing practice of overcoming technical hurdles and of increasingly controlling the world. Geoengineers want to impose human power over the atmosphere in the service of "dewilding" the climate system. Similarly, so-called de-extinctionists want to reverse biodiversity loss by taking over the process of evolution. They propose synthesizing genetic material from extinct species and inserting it into contemporary living relatives. In this way they hope to bring back, say, the woolly mammoth or the aurochs. They see such efforts as simply another chapter in humanity's quest for greater mastery. In both instances, the idea is to extend human reach to the Earth's inner workings. The globe, for geoengineers and de-extinctionists, is simply the next frontier on which to impose human influence.

As will become clear, this book argues the opposite. Instead of trying to extend humanity's reach to the furthest ends of the Earth—instead of "dewilding" the planet as a whole—I argue for "rewilding" human experience. This means inviting *more* unpredictability, inconvenience, and even danger into our lives. It involves turning off the impulse to control everything that escapes our dictates and opening up to difference and vulnerability—especially the vulnerability of others (including nonhuman creatures). In this latter sense, rewilding invites us to see otherness as a gift rather than something to brace against or subjugate; and it teaches us to appreciate the way other people and nonhuman beings move to their own beat. In other words, rewilding requires that we get out of our comfort zones and develop understanding and compassion as an act of global response. In this capacity, rewilding serves two purposes. First, it diffuses some of the pressure that fuels planetary challenges. By retracting the impulse to control everything, it acts like a relief valve on brave new wildness. Second, it enhances the quality of our lives. We are currently living through a moment of acute environmental intensification. How will we comport ourselves and relate to one another as the world spins out of control? Rewilding offers a strategy and ethic for these trying times.

2

Wild Modernity

Global wildness begins not with a bang but a grin. It lurches forward as we turn an ignition key, twist a faucet, thumbprint an iPhone, or jot down a thought on a sticky note. It is seemingly innocent enough. No one wants to unleash craziness on the world. It comes about from countless tiny daily decisions. It happens, at least at one level, as people simply move minute by minute through their days, seeking a sense of comfort.

As I sit here typing in late November in the northern hemisphere, I feel a slight chill. My shoulders are tightening and my feet are growing cold. I could put on more clothes, but I'd feel cramped in multiple layers. It's easier to turn up the thermostat. Likewise, I want to invite a friend to dinner. I could walk a few miles to their house, but it's much easier just to whip out a cell phone. So it goes with everything. I want a cup of tea, more light in the room, or to know who has sent an email. I push, flick, and click, *et voilà*, I'm satisfied—at least until the next desire. It is as if I had an infinite series of itches and I reached out to the electrified, resourced, affluent world to scratch them. I have no desire to hurt or make things worse for anyone; I'm simply trying to adjust the world to fit my wishes.

With each move, however, the world does not simply shift. It shudders. To satisfy my desires, I am essentially sticking a straw into the Earth—including into other communities—and sucking out the insides. I'm digging a coal mine, pulling up a tree, slurping from a river, or giving the planet an enema to release natural gas. I'm also extracting labor, setting into motion exploitative short-term practices among economically strapped communities, and reproducing long-term structures of power that determine resource use. Each time, the Earth gives. It finds the means to regenerate a steady stream of resources—a process that often requires that people squeeze themselves that much more and dig deeper into the planet's natural bounty. The Earth also finds the ability to absorb my waste. Each time I reach for a cracker, plug in a computer, vacuum a rug, or discard a plastic bottle I point the other end of the straw into the atmosphere, across the land, inside other people's lives, or back into the oceans, and expect whatever I release to disappear. Again, I mean no harm. I'm simply living my life. Or, more accurately, I am simply living my *comfortable* life, as Aldo Leopold might say (1989, p. 71).

The problem is, I'm not alone. Not only are most of the 7.7 billion other people also seeking convenience and well-being, but worldwide commercial, political, and cultural forces peddle ease and consumption as an engine of corporate and state wealth, a route to personal happiness, and an answer to many societal challenges. This means that I make my choices not in a private vacuum but am largely instrumentalized by wider structures of power. To put it perhaps simplistically, when I choose convenience, I am operating as an appendage to global forces, largely capitalist, which thrive on producing an economy of comfort. Not only has capitalism discovered the profit potential of selling ease; it has also standardized patterns of consumption that revolve around what sociologist Elizabeth Shove (2003) describes as "comfort, cleanliness, and convenience." It has ritualized showers, heating, air conditioning, clothes' washing, car driving, and other, relatively recently normalized practices that prize expediency and demand an exponential offering of products, services, and energy. Such products are advertised as necessary tools for mitigating nuisance and discomfort in the daily lives of affluent consumers. Importantly, this is happening also because capital accumulation enables corporate entities to hold so much power that they end up determining societal choices—such as today's commitment to fossil fuel economies. Historian Jason Moore (2015) highlights this when he argues that, in the contemporary world, capitalism is not an accessory—one that simply organizes economic life—but the central principle that organizes *all* life. It literally forms the socio-biophysical conditions of life itself. It does so by ensuring that wealth constitutes the main source of social, political, and cultural power, and this means that extractivism—exercised on people, other creatures, and the Earth itself—becomes a way of global life (Klein, 2014).

There are, of course, plenty of critical voices trying to disentangle from structures of power and many people are experimenting with alternative forms of economic production and exchange. They remind us that, deep down, economic growth is not an answer to the world's problems, material accumulation fails to produce lasting happiness, and consumption stems more from corporate greed than from individual preferences. But the sheer extensiveness and concentrated power of the consumptive machine muffle critics. What was once merely a western way of life has gone global. There is virtually no community unattached to the world economy, global markets, and the compelling cultural message to consume. These days, everyone has a straw into the Earth and other people's lives and, while the wealthy slurp and the poor barely sip, almost everyone draws from it with force, passion, and a sense of entitlement.

Ageless Antipathy

Convenience, comfort, and capitalism are not the whole story. In fact, they come at the tail end. They represent merely the capillaries of a long historical process and the expression of a deeper human impulse. Brave new wildness has been long in the coming and deep in humanity's bones. It stems from an age-old antipathy toward the unknown, unpredictable, and irascible qualities of experience.

Environmental historian Roderick Nash suggests that, before the agricultural revolution, humans lived on undifferentiated land (Nash, 2014). As hunter-gatherers, they moved from one region to another, without there being any conceptual or physical boundary to demarcate them from the wider world around them. People shared space and constantly interacted with plants, other animals, and the elements. There was no human realm distinct from nature, no place that humans could call their very own. To the degree that people felt at home, they did so as being part of the wider realm of rivers, mountains, deserts, forests, and other creatures. One might say that hunter-gatherers lived permanently "outside." This meant that they were constantly subject to, and built lives around, the vicissitudes of nature.

This changed over the long unfolding of the agricultural revolution. By one account, agriculture provided a modicum of stability, which fostered more complex, sedentary communities; and these carved out what could be thought of as "indoor" space. Within the boundaries of settlements, granaries enabled people to plant crops year after year, and domesticated cows, pigs, sheep, and dogs provided both a steady diet of protein and a reliable supply of work animals. People built shelters that shielded them from wind, snow, and heat. Within their walls, settlements created a sphere of partial reliability, control, and safety that had eluded earlier nomadic peoples. Agricultural sedentarism cordoned off a realm wherein people could live with a greater sense of collective stability and protection. It offered a space that insulated them from the wider, erratic world. It created an "inside" amid the broader "outside."

The agricultural revolution not only circumscribed a human space, but concomitantly defined what lay beyond human community. If early settlements provided a degree of safety, beyond their borders were the wilds—the domain of otherness. This is where the ways of nature rather than those of humans presided. Beyond the last patch of cultivated land or human dwelling, the world operated according to its own processes, indifferent to the whims and efforts of people. When people ventured out into the wild—to hunt, gather food, or explore—they left the confines of patterned and somewhat contrived living and entered a less known and less predictable space. According to Nash (2014), this was the beginning of the idea of "wilderness." Wilderness was what lay beyond human community. It was the domain of the untamed. Over millennia, the concept of wilderness would assume different meanings and people would have different kinds of relationships with it. But the boundary those first farmers etched onto the landscape created a sense of insulation between the human and the non-human worlds and set up a long-standing antagonism between the two.

Much of this drama was driven by fear. As

settlements grew and became associated with security, the outside seemed increasingly dangerous. Its otherness promised inconsistency, difference, danger, and challenge. Importantly, this became the case not only with nature but also other settlements. While intergroup violence predates the agricultural revolution, tribal conflict between agricultural settlements was widespread. Indeed, evidence suggests that systemic warfare, in contrast to occasional massacres, arose during the era of Neolithic sedentarism (Heath, 2017). Communities fought over stored grains, fertile soil, reliable water sources. This suggests that, as communities draw boundaries, everything beyond their walls assumes a menacing character. The wildness of nature and wildness of other people share a resonance. This is one reason why people, since the agricultural revolution, have constantly pushed the boundaries of the inside outward. They have wanted to protect themselves from the unknown and have done so by overtaking it. In this sense, for several thousand years, there has been a persistent sense of fear of and battle against wildness—human and otherwise.

An alternative narrative of the agricultural revolution makes the same point, but in a different way. Recent scholarship has shown that people did not voluntarily enclose land and enter into agricultural settlements in search of greater stability but were forced to do so. As early settlements arose here and there, leaders recognized that agricultural sedentarism allowed social stratification and, for some, the ability to avoid the drudgery and precariousness of subsistence living—whether as hunter-gatherers or as farmers toiling in fields. In other words, they saw agricultural sedentarism as a route to their own power, comfort, and security. As political scientist James Scott (2017) argues, this move on the part of early elites represents the embryonic emergence of the modern state. To Scott, the agricultural revolution was not an inevitable chapter in humanity's cultural evolution but an administrative choice that boosted the welfare of some over others. Agricultural sedentarism—especially the production of cereal grains that could be stored, counted, and, importantly, taxed—generated wealth for elites and facilitated the consolidation of power. This enabled domestication—not just of plants and animals but also of people. The administrative arm of agricultural communities forcibly collected and often enslaved people near centers of power and demanded the production of crop surpluses in an early effort at state-building.

According to this account, agricultural settlements were not beacons of protection and stability but dens of fragility, exploitation, and brutality. They were fragile in that communities relied on a narrow, geographically circumscribed diet that often failed to provide a full range of nutrients and was vulnerable to blights and the precarious fate of specific lands. People would have been better off living as hunter-gatherers who supplemented their diets with grains rather than building their lives solely around a grain economy. Agricultural settlements were oppressive in that the nascent state apparatus depended upon forced labor and lived off its fruits. For early farmers, existence was anything but safe and comfortable under the harsh, unjust regimes they were subject to. Far from insulating people from unpredictability and danger, the agricultural revolution built its own kind of wildness within the walls of communities. It exacerbated a type of social wildness wherein lives became more precarious as most people were exposed to the vulnerabilities of living in one place and subject to the violence perpetrated by administrative elites.

Notwithstanding this, the more critical account of the agricultural revolution still explains the age-old effort to stamp out wildness—to reduce uncertainty and mitigate dangers that emanated from the other, the unknown, and the uncontrollable. It shows how the more powerful agriculturalists were able to effect their own security on the backs of others. To do so, they had to suppress the otherness of hunter-gatherers and pastoralists; they had to beat out any resistance to their own wills. The more critical account of the agricultural revolution locates the antipathy toward wildness not only at the interface between people, the elements, and other creatures but at the interface between people themselves. Using language introduced earlier, Scott and others describe how the agricultural revolution pushed wildness "horizontally"—from the lives of the privileged into the lives of the less fortunate. This push is an ancient expression of fearing and battling wildness.

Modern War on Wildness

The impulse to tame wildness may stretch back to the agricultural revolution (or perhaps even earlier: see Scott, 2017) but the justification and means for doing so emerged most fully in the modern era—the cultural period that began in medieval Europe roughly in the seventeenth century and continues today. In premodern times, when people tried to minimize the erratic elements of life, their efforts were limited by a lack of knowledge, tools, and engineering muscle. They could work at the margins to shape general conditions, but they never believed they had the right or possessed the means actually to rule over the conditions themselves. Mastery over the unpredictable, risky elements in life was the domain of God or providence—not human beings. Modernity represents a break from this understanding and the institutional structures that supported it. A combination of Enlightenment thinking, scientific and technological innovation, industrialization, and growing capitalist production paved the way for recognizing that one need not be subject to nature's capriciousness or the cyclical pattern of life that denies a person control over their destiny. As historian Peter Bernstein (1996, p. 1) puts it, "[t]he revolutionary idea that defines the boundary between modern times and the past is the mastery of risk: the notion that the future is more than a whim of the gods and that men and women are not passive before nature."

Central to taking responsibility for one's fate is the place of reason in modern life. Modern thinking privileges rationality. Early on, this opened the way for humans to have enough confidence to penetrate and decipher the seeming mysteries of the natural world and to begin systematically taming not simply the hinterlands that lay beyond established communities but also the wildness that courses through all life. Knowledge was seen as a weapon against superstition, ignorance, and customary ways of doing things, and with knowledge came an increasing ability to manipulate and control human experience. This happened as the natural sciences grew in their ability to analyze biological, physical, and chemical dynamics, and as the technical arts gained confidence and capability to translate scientific understanding into material application. Along with this, the social sciences arose and began deciphering the structures of collective life. This, in parallel with new networks of commerce, power, and culture, gave rise to the modern state and bureaucratic and institutional mechanisms aimed at better ordering and more effectively governing society. It also enabled the emergence of capitalist modes of production and, eventually, the globalization of economic affairs—which has dramatically concentrated power and revved up the ability to bend nature and society to human design. Together, these provided the capability for pushing the boundaries of human inquiry and shaping the world to fit human aspirations. At the heart of this transformation was a shared commitment to banish wildness. This commitment, like that of earlier agriculturalists, sprang from a quasi innate antipathy to what is unwieldy and from a belief that controlling others—people as well as plants, animals, and land—lends greater predictability and security to one's own life.

The modern war on wildness gained momentum from an emerging mechanistic view, which offered ethical justification to "bound [nature] into service," as English philosopher Francis Bacon put it (quoted in Spretnak, 2012, p. 54). The rise of the sciences and the perfecting of engineering rested on seeing the world more as a set of objects that obeyed unalterable laws than as an organic, living set of interdependent organisms. Gone was the understanding that animals, plants, or weather patterns have intrinsic meaning or agency. Lightning happens not because gods will it or because of some internal purpose but because electrically charged storm systems produce sparks. Likewise, seasons change not as part of a divinely created cyclical process but simply because the Earth's proximity to heat and light changes as the planet revolves around the sun. Plants grow not with purpose, but merely in response to sunlight; and animals behave according to instinct—they lack developed consciousness. Indeed, the whole panoply of the more-than-human world—the realm beyond human control, the realm of wildness—gets flattened in modern times.

Modernity bleaches out the subjectivity of nature.

Once the world is seen as a matter of mindless mechanics, people can do with it as they please; and this further justifies efforts to push into and eradicate wildness. Objects—or, more accurately, mechanisms—have no soul, will, or cognizance. As such, they are undeserving of ethical regard. This is why the modern philosopher René Descartes could justify vivisection: according to his understanding, animals, being devoid of subjectivity, feel no pain. The cries and whimpers one hears when dissecting a live animal are merely the squeaks of mechanical wheels turning in response to stimuli (Mueller, 2017, p. 13). This is also why billions of people today can comfortably ignore the mistreatment of farm animals, decimation of indigenous plants, and oversaturation of the atmosphere with carbon. Animals, plants, and certainly air seemingly have no subjectivity, and thus no intrinsic worth. They represent mere matter that operates according to physical laws or biological instinct and, as such, can be used indiscriminately for human purposes. Put differently, the modern mechanistic view removes interiority from the more-than-human realm, and this further empowers humans in their perennial battle with wildness.

Much of the move from an organic to a mechanical

view of nature turned on changing understandings of gender. The organic viewpoint suggested that, metaphorically, the Earth was a nurturing mother that provided resources and fostered human well-being (Merchant, 1990). This encouraged respect and, consequently, cultural constraint. The Earth was alive, sensitive, and beneficent, and should be treated accordingly. By turning the Earth into a dead set of resources and replacing organicism with mechanism, modern science did not disperse with a gendered understanding of nature so much as sanctioned a more interrogating and exploitative orientation toward the female Earth. Bacon, Descartes, and other progenitors of modern science depicted the femaleness of the Earth as a wild, uncontrollable force that had to be investigated and mined; and Earth itself, like a woman, had to be reduced to psychic and reproductive resources. According to ecofeminist Carolyn Merchant, modern patriarchy and mechanism worked hand in hand to bolster control and domination.

Modernity has facilitated an orientation of supremacy not simply to women but people in general. It is no accident that the most extensive form of colonization happened in the modern era. The instrumental rationality that separated and lifted humans above all else also prioritized certain human communities, rendering select people less fully human than others, and thus susceptible to mechanisms of control and exploitation. The colonial experience—wherein European powers thrust themselves into "uncivilized" areas by taking imperial control over the so-called natives—represents the epitome of this process. To be sure, there were economic, technological, and political reasons for European colonization. At a minimum, people of the metropole sought to obtain greater amounts of power, security, and comfort by enslaving and exploiting others and therewith displace wildness out of their own lives. But at the heart of the enterprise was also an ethical calculation of moral worth. The people in the hinterlands—lacking industry and seemingly mature culture—seemed a notch below Europeans of the metropole. Ironically, this was partly because they did not try or simply could not succeed in controlling the world around them. Apparently stuck in their customary ways and representing a fundamentally different kind of creature, the colonized were ripe for imperial control. They were considered undeserving of equal moral treatment and thus could be used as slaves or arms of the imperial economy; or they were merely ignored, as colonizers plundered their lands and labor.

The legacy of colonialism remains. Power

dynamics still rely on differential levels of moral worth and contemporary forms of production and cultural reproduction place certain people at the receiving end of practices that enhance the lives of some at the expense of others. The privileged often ignore, or at least implicitly delimit, the subjectivity of others and this rationalizes different forms of moral treatment. This is especially the case as the division of labor, assembly lines, specialization, and complex modes of production hide the lived experience of laborers or as the mesmerizing entertainments of affluent culture conceal the lives of those who are unable to support themselves. In this sense, the modern mechanical view is a matter of bleaching out not just the interiority of the more-than-human world, but very much human interiority as well. This explains why certain communities find themselves disproportionately affected by environmental harm and why one enduring dimension of racism and sexism entails using nature as a medium of oppression (Bullard, 2000; Agyeman, 2005; Taylor, 2014). It also allows for widespread extractivism and thus provides a key engine for eradicating wildness.

Modernity, of course, is not homogenous. Plenty of people have rejected modernity's primary assumptions over the past few hundred years and continue to do so today. Many hold a more organic view of nature and prize ways of knowing and interacting with the world beyond the strict bounds of rationality. They also reject patriarchy, colonialism, and the demeaning and exploitative practice of extractivism applied on other people. One sees this, in a general way, in romanticism and similarly minded movements of earlier centuries—movements wherein people worried that instrumental rationality would diminish emotions or affective sensibilities and questioned mechanistic views of the world. Critical thinkers witnessed and resisted industrialism's expansive reworking of nature and human interaction. They lamented denuded forests, polluted skies, and tainted waters as well as the exploitation of labor, as capitalism grew and intensified along with the Industrial Revolution and as slavery marked so much of the colonial experience. These thinkers expressed concerns about modernity's attitude to nature and unpredictability. They recognized that taming wildness had its excesses; it could overshoot its own intentions. It may create more comfortable conditions for many but, in the act of doing so, it oppressed others and desecrated the very source of well-being. Thinkers who expressed such views saw wildness not as an enemy but an ally. Indeed, many thinkers, such as poet William Wordsworth, philosopher Ralph Emerson, and naturalist Alexander von Humboldt, regarded it as essential to human flourishing. In their view, wildness offered a realm of encounter that opened people to vaster horizons of emotional, philosophical, and spiritual experience. It provided a frontier against which one could appreciate one's own limits, the narrow bandwidth of day-to-day understanding, and even one's mortality. It proffered a testing ground for human courage and an opportunity for cultural interaction. In a different way, thinkers have also valued wildness specifically for its otherness beyond even human encounter. Wildness represents the *more-than*-human world—a realm outside the human domain—that possesses intrinsic value. Its existence is essential to the panoply of earthly life and important to humans, even if they have no direct contact with it (Mueller, 2017). In all these ways, thinkers agreed with Thoreau when he famously wrote that "wildness is the preservation of the world" (1992, p. 644); and the sentiment has resonated with many ever since. It gave rise to much of the modern environmental movement. Indeed, environmentalism of the 1960s and 1970s gave contemporary expression to a more Earth-appreciating understanding that has long existed alongside—but, importantly, in the shadow of—the modern, rationalist, mechanistic view.

Wild Modernity

Modernity's critics may have deepened reflection on the purpose and consequences of humanity's war on wildness and created intellectual pockets of critical thought. They may also have left a legacy of sensitive environmental thought and action. However, they did not stem the tide. The modernist machine rolled right over them. This is unsurprising. People have been thrusting the tentacles of the "inside" world outward at least since the agricultural revolution—across cultures and various terrains as well as into the air, water, and soil. Modernity has accelerated and intensified this process. Its spirit and material capability have left no domain untouched by humanity's manipulative fingers. Anyone who benefits now from the comforts created by human ingenuity and extensive control of the planet is a child of the modern era. Likewise, many who suffer the indignities of oppression and control are the recipients of modernity's intensified antipathy toward otherness and its perfection of rationalizing and controlling human affairs. Modernity has delivered on the age-old dream of human supremacy and the ability of some to gain comfort and security by controlling others. It has provided not only greater justification but also the material conditions for stamping out wildness.

3

Wild Climate

Many elements of modernity solidified human dominance over wildness. One, however, proved essential. This is the commercial use of fossil fuels. Humans have used coal, oil, and even natural gas for thousands of years to cook, heat, and light up their lives. However, it wasn't until the mid-1800s, when they learned how to drill for oil, run steam engines on coal, and more effectively capture and transport natural gas, that the full potential of fossil fuels began to be realized. Commercial fossil fuel use, predominantly coal, essentially created and drove the Industrial Revolution. It catapulted the world into a profoundly new era.

In a very general sense, one could say that humans turned to fossil fuels to make life more secure and easier. Before the Industrial Revolution, even the richest people lived and worked in cold, dark buildings and were subject to the availability of wood for cooking. Journalist Charles Mann explains how winter visitors to Versailles in 1695 had to wear fur at dinner and drank iced water because the wood fireplaces failed to keep the palace comfortably warm. He likewise describes how Monticello was typically so cold in the winter that Jefferson's inkwell often froze (Mann, 2018, p. 256). These discomforts changed dramatically with the introduction of fossil fuels. A hundred years after Jefferson's death, large numbers of people were able to heat as well as light their entire homes. This advance had a huge impact on well-being, not only because people could feel more comfortable in the winter and take advantage of more light in the evening, but also because it enabled central plumbing (since pipes no longer froze), which created the conditions for modern cooking and sanitation. Fossil fuels also made possible commercial electricity, which then drove industrialization itself and now powers the thousand and one gadgets that populate contemporary privileged life. At a more general level, fossil fuels made possible faster transportation systems (with the advent of steamships, railroads, and eventually automobiles) and the infrastructure for contemporary urban life (with the mass production of steel and cement). Today, for most people, there is not an element of life that is not tied in some way to fossil fuels. As Mann puts it, "[t]he impact of fossil fuels exhausts hyperbole" (2018, p. 255).

From many perspectives, fossil fuels have been a godsend. Their widespread use has incontrovertibly enhanced life for many. The rise of fossil fuels correlates with greater nutrition, income, longevity, and productivity at the individual level. In the aggregate, hydrocarbons radically accelerated economic growth, population increase, technological innovation, and cultural evolution. In all of this, oil, gas, and coal have enabled people to limit the threats and discomforts of life; they have strengthened humanity's hand in controlling the world. This has not necessarily led to greater happiness—although even this most difficult measure of well-being may be associated with fossil fuels—but has created large havens of security and ease that few would give up, once they have experienced them. One sees this reflected in both small and large ways.

Think for a moment about driving a car or flying in a plane. Before automobiles or airplanes, people had to walk, ride a horse, or sail a ship to travel or haul goods. In doing so, they had to confront and deal with the various challenges inherent in being exposed to the elements and in facing threats from other people, wild animals, and uncontrollable seas.

Travel involved significant unpredictability; one constantly moved through unknown areas and carried little with them to make the journey safe and comfortable.

Enter fossil fuels and combustion engines. These not only increased the distance one could travel but also got rid of many dangers, resistances, and inconveniences. They tamed the frontier and domesticated travel. The car, for instance, provides the chance to move through the world in an insulated machine, often outfitted with heating, cooling, lighting, entertainment, and in some cases even driverless steering. One can be autonomous, travel at fast speeds, and insulate oneself from the elements and other people. When one is driving, the environment is essentially unnoticeable. This is even more dramatic with airplanes. Sitting in one's reserved seat, a passenger may as well be sitting in a room with a favorite book or personal media machine, invulnerable to the many hazards and nuisances of earlier kinds of travel. Planes represent a conquest of space, an upper hand on time, and a technological feat that renders indifferent bodies of water, expanses of land, and even currents of air. Fueled by oil, they remove travelers from most immediate risks and inconveniences.

Fossil fuels do this with every deployment. By

turning darkness to light or cold to heat, they free people from nature's vicissitudes; by enabling the transport of food from around the world, they liberate one from the seasons; by making possible the manufacturing of cement and steel, they allow people to construct buildings and other types of infrastructure that undergird and protect towns and cities; and by fueling the Internet and delivery trucks, they allow people to avoid even the small annoyances of dealing with neighbors, since many can now order almost anything online and have it delivered to their door. Fossil fuels relax the world. They minimize the unpredictability that comes from being subject to the ways of nature or other people. To hark back to an earlier point, fossil fuels allow people to push the boundaries of the 'inside' outward. They enable people to encroach upon and increasingly control the world around them.

Fossil fuels came to dominance not simply because they fulfilled a functional need but also because they could be subject to capture, and thus harnessed by those seeking greater power and control over others. Seen in this way, the transition to fossil fueled economies—like the shift from hunting-gathering to agriculturalism—happened not simply as a matter of course, but as a deliberate strategy of power accumulation. As a number of scholars have pointed out, the move from traditional sources of power like water and wind to coal and oil was specifically engineered to enhance power and control by some over others. For instance, geographer Andreas Malm, in his extraordinarily sophisticated work *Fossil Capital* (Malm 2016), explains that the transition to coal took place not because it allowed increasing numbers of people to mitigate danger and inconvenience but because coal provided a superior way to accumulate capital, concentrate production, and control labor. When first introduced as a source of industrial power (rather than simply for heating), coal was more expensive than waterpower and required investments unavailable to traditional mills or cotton manufacturers. Nonetheless, coal offered a type of "stock energy" that could be stored, moved, and deployed in ways that articulated well with growing capitalism. Most importantly, by powering steam, it led to mechanization, which reduced the need to support and manage large numbers of laborers and concentrated production within factories, an arena within which workers could be more easily controlled. Indeed, Malm claims that the emergence of steam power as the bedrock of industrialism was partly a response to industrial militancy in the early 1800s in England. Steam power offered a way to liberate production from over-reliance on unruly laborers. Coal provided a tool for the owners of production to dispense with, or at least better control, the necessary but "othered" agents of production. Far from seeing fossil fuels as an answer to public demand for more comfort, Malm offers a productivist explanation, focused more on the dynamism of capitalism—and, I would add, on the comfort aspirations of capitalists.

Political scientist Timothy Mitchell (2011) makes a similar point about the emergence of fossil fuels. He too advances a productivist account that reinforces how fossil fuels get enlisted by industrialists to pursue strategic aims—and thus battle their own struggles with wildness—rather than serve as a panacea for society's energy needs and a public desire to mitigate discomfort. Like Malm, Mitchell acknowledges the importance of coal in spurring the Industrial Revolution. In his reading, however, coal proved less effective than Malm acknowledges in liberating energy production from workers. While more concentrated than water mills, coal production relied on extensive networks made up of mining, loading, transporting, and consuming; and these provided multiple sites susceptible to worker sabotage, strikes, and disruption. Coal thus offered opportunities for workers to demand better pay, more conducive working conditions, and protected rights. Mitchell points out that this generated greater pressure for democratic aspirations.

In the mid-twentieth century, oil emerged as a perfect antidote to democratic pressure. Produced initially, and still predominantly, in the non-democratic Middle East, cheap and abundant oil distances energy infrastructure from the clawing arms of mass, democratic publics. Although Mitchell doesn't use Malm's vocabulary, oil is more "flow" than "stock" energy. It moves through pipelines and transporting it requires fewer stages staffed by workers. In short, Mitchell, like Malm, rejects the notion that oil and, by extension, fossil fuels emerged as a benign energy source to which humanity turned for greater comfort and to mitigate wildness. Rather he underlines how they served and continue to serve strategic choices of elites seeking their own, parochial aims at power and how they disempowered those who stood in elites' way.

A productivist understanding may qualify, but nevertheless still bolsters, the general point about how oil, gas, and coal have served as means to mitigate wildness. Like agriculturalists in relation to hunter-gatherers, the barons of the fossil fuel industry engaged in their own form of control. They shared a widespread antipathy toward otherness and sought to build lives immune from nature's and society's exigencies. By accumulating power and using it to rule over or at least control others, they turned their own "inside" out. They colonized the world around them. The reward was lives of privilege that sidestepped, overcame, or otherwise avoided the cramping, annoying, and disruptive activities of others, both in one's commercial and in one's personal life. In the process, elites disseminated the wildness around them horizontally. This is how fossil-fueled privilege banishes wildness. As Malm, Mitchell, and others suggest, it certainly does so for industrial elites. As more conventional thinkers explain, it also does so for large segments of the world's population—those best able to take advantage of fossil fuels' energy gifts.

Hacking the Global Carbon Cycle

Fossil fuels may have created havens of security for certain people but, in the main and from a more global perspective, they haven't gotten rid of wildness so much as amplified and displaced it. They have moved it not only horizontally but vertically— to the planet as a whole. Climate change represents its own kind of wildness—a type that is not only more ferocious but ultimately more extensive and terrifying owing to the concentrated and accumulative dynamics involved. The buildup of carbon dioxide and other greenhouse gases (GHG) in the atmosphere introduces an Earth-rattling form of wildness manifest in calving glaciers, intensified storms, unprecedented heatwaves, increased wildfires, and cascading ecological decline. It is as if the cost of local safety and comfort has come at a global price. The privileged can drive where they want, eat food from the far corners of the world, and enjoy the comforts of heating and cooling. However, underneath such security, the planet itself is reeling. Fossil fuels have made life safer for many, but unleashed a brave new and irascible wildness skyward.

The sheer amount of carbon dioxide and other GHGs accumulating in the atmosphere is altering the Earth's climate and inducing planetary instability. For millennia and up until the Industrial Revolution, atmospheric carbon concentrations were fairly stable and oscillated within a relatively narrow bandwidth of 270–90 parts per million (ppm). These conditions made possible the flourishing of all kinds of life. These days, atmospheric carbon dioxide (CO_2) concentrations exceed 415 ppm (Daily CO_2, 2019) and this is throwing the

Earth's carbon cycle off kilter as the Earth enters a fundamentally new climate era. (To be sure, atmospheric carbon levels have fluctuated throughout geologic time, but have not topped 400 ppm for the past several million years; see Jones, 2017.)

Through carbon and other GHG emissions, humans have imprinted the Earth's operations; but they have little control over the impact of the signature. Put differently, they have tinkered with the planetary infrastructure, which makes life possible, but have little clue about how to steer such fiddling in stable, life-enhancing directions. They have essentially thrown a wrench into the background conditions of life and unleashed a wildness that, in its accumulative form, now threatens planetary integrity.

Climate wildness is well underway. It is a universal, existential threat that grows exponentially in magnitude every year. Today everything that was frozen on Earth is melting; sea levels are rising; storms are intensifying; wildfires are more prevalent and severe; heat waves have become more punishing; and innumerable species are disappearing as areas turn hotter. On top of this, positive feedback loops are amplifying and accelerating climate change. Thawing permafrost releases increasing amounts of methane; expanding wildfires discharge greater amounts of CO_2; and sea ice melt reduces the amount of sunlight that is reflected back into space and thus leads to more warming of the oceans (and more ice melt). Socially, feedbacks are also intensifying. Almost every adaptation to changing conditions creates a greater need for energy and, since most energy these days comes from fossil fuels, we are locked into a vicious circle of responding to more climate discomfort by using more of the very sources that created and exacerbate climate change. Hotter weather encourages the use of additional air conditioning; dwindling freshwater spurs desalinization; and damaging storms require more material resources to be used in rebuilding. These loops feed the climate system and intensify the wild character of climate change. They give further expression to the vertical aspect of fossil-fueled comfort.

The horizontal dimension has to do with how climate wildness etches itself into the world. Yes, emissions float into the atmosphere and thus "move up" and infect global climate. However, the dynamics involved also disseminate laterally, extending across societies such that the effects of climate change fall upon specific people who live in particular places; and the pattern of such effect is highly uneven. This pattern involves not simply the social stratification associated with the erection of fossil fuel production infrastructure, but the specifics of mining, processing, and transporting fossil fuels and their eventual lodging in the atmosphere. For instance, those working and living near coal mines, oil refineries, or hydraulic fracturing facilities live with contaminated water, polluted air, despoiled landscapes, and increased earthquakes. Living in what is often called "sacrificed zones" (Lerner, 2010), these people are at the forefront of extractivism and thus bear the brunt of fossil fuels' damaging effects. Sadly, these same people—usually poor, nonwhite, and politically marginalized—suffer at the other end too, as fossil fuels are burned. They live on the most fragile lands and in substandard structures, and lack robust means to protect themselves and social welfare networks that could help them recover from climate-related disasters. This is particularly troubling, since the people who least contribute to climate change—those with small carbon footprints—suffer the bulk of its damaging effects. For them, hydrocarbons have not gotten rid of but rather have intensified the wild character of their lives.

The vertical and horizontal dimensions of climate change reveal the fungible and unjust character of trying to get rid of wildness. The dangers and discomforts of wildness do not disappear when people put the screws to them; they simply move. They spread out into other people's lives and onto the planet as a whole. When they do so, they take on a more intractable character, since confronting them in their accumulative and global form is much more challenging. Not only are heat waves, wildfires, melting polar regions, and tumbling biological depletion nonlinear and erratic in their unfolding; the social mechanisms charged with responding to such conditions are ill-equipped to tame climate change or otherwise bring it under control.

In 1992 countries negotiated the United Nations Framework Convention on Climate Change (UNFCCC). The Convention established an agenda for ensuring the stabilization of "greenhouse gas concentrations in the atmosphere at a level that would prevent dangerous anthropogenic interference with the climate system" (UNFCCC, 1992). At the time, atmospheric carbon concentrations stood at 356 ppm, and the world was emitting roughly 22.2 gigatons per year (World Bank Group, 2019). Almost thirty years later, after countries committed to reducing GHG emissions through the Kyoto Protocol, Paris Accord, and other agreements, concentrations now stand, as mentioned, at over 415 ppm and the world emits almost twice the amount of carbon it emitted in 1992. Furthermore, as 80 percent of the world's energy demands are met by fossil fuels and world energy demand is estimated to grow by 27 percent between now and 2040, it is almost certain that these figures will increase (Eule, 2019). Far from stabilizing GHG concentrations, the world is multiplying them. Mitigating climate change seems, at best, a distant dream. Any sober assessment must acknowledge that the world is experiencing runaway climate change, with no end in sight and with plenty of wild feedback loops to exacerbate and accelerate its terrifying effects.

Climate change will grow out of control still further simply as a result of all the oil, gas, and coal currently slated to be burned. At the 2015 climate meeting in Paris, the international community agreed to keep global temperatures ideally below a 1.5 C degree increase from pre-industrial levels, and certainly no higher than 2 C degrees. In order to stay within these limits, the world should emit only a certain amount of additional CO_2 into the atmosphere. This represents the world's carbon budget. Although numbers are imprecise, it is well known that fossil fuel companies (and states that act like them) possess at least five times that amount, in proven reserves (McKibben, 2012). Given the unlikelihood that companies will voluntarily—or even under duress—write off such reserves as stranded assets, it appears inevitable that the world will burn through both the 1.5 and 2 C degree thresholds relatively soon. One estimate predicts surpassing the 1.5 C degree mark by 2030 (McKibben, 2019, p. 15). The sheer pressure to mine and burn reserves highlights the relative ungovernability of mitigation efforts.

The inability to get a handle on climate change stems from many sources. Those tracking the carbon budget and commercial reserves point to overwhelming economic incentives to extract and burn hydrocarbons at the highest possible rate. Indeed, no amount of warning about climate change has convinced fossil fuel companies to scale back their commercial efforts beyond mere window dressing. If anything, the warnings have succeeded in making the fossil fuel industry work harder to divert public attention from the scientific evidence of anthropogenic climate change. ExxonMobil, for instance, has long known about the dangers of climate change but kept such information from its shareholders and the public for years (Hall, 2015; Oreskes and Conway, 2011). This was part of a broader effort by the industry to sow doubt about climate science. Such economic incentives are so powerful that they often instrumentalize the very governments that have committed to reducing

GHG emissions. Governments all over the world—even the most climate-committed—are either relaxing regulations on carbon emissions or simply admitting that they cannot achieve their nationally determined contributions while concomitantly seeking economic growth. This is partly a consequence of governments' promising their citizens economic development and believing that climate protection has unacceptable economic costs; but it is also a result of industry pressure. Climate is hostage to systematic lobbying and global regulatory capture by fossil fuel producers. More broadly and stated differently, climate is going wild because of capitalist dynamics (Klein, 2014).

At a different level, climate change is out of control because of structural factors that have to do with the political organization of the world. *States* signed the UNFCCC and have participated in international diplomatic efforts to mitigate GHGs. They are the sole parties to the Convention and to all subsequent accords. The problem is that states possess sovereignty only over circumscribed territory. In an anarchical world order that lacks a single universal authority, states are on their own to secure their national interests and are often blind or resistant to taking significant collective action. In other words there is a structural mismatch between the scope of the problem and the governmental mechanisms that are available to respond. Climate change respects no national boundaries; it is global in scope; it is unitary in quality. States, on the other hand, are fragmentary units concerned primarily with their own, territorially bounded well-being. They will enter into agreements and undertake collective commitments when they see actual benefits for themselves, or when the costs are relatively low; but they will shrink from such commitments when benefits are less obvious or perceived costs are substantial. This mismatch, which is fundamental to addressing any global challenge, puts climate mitigation still further out of reach. The international state system is ill-equipped to crack down on a problem that emerges across the world, imposes disproportionate costs, and whose solution requires coordinated, collective effort—with little to no free riding. This condition, famously known as the "tragedy of the commons," ensures that governments will constantly fall short in their efforts to tame the roaring amassment of climate change. The state system encourages *national* safety and security at the expense of *global* wilding.

Beyond the economy and governments, climate will continue to remain out of control for cultural reasons. Almost all economies these days are at least quasi-capitalist and premised on ever-expanding material consumption. Indeed, consumerism is the global motif. As many people around the world have become more affluent, they have understandably come to see happiness and success tied to material acquisition. Consumerism, as a cultural phenomenon, arose after World War II in the West. It was initially an effort to sustain a war-pressed economy and turn the war machine into a mechanism of continued economic growth. Since then, consumerism has infiltrated the minds of people in most of the global North and been disseminated around the world. Researchers such as Erik Assadourian (2013) liken current consumerism to a globalized religion. To many, consumerism provides a *raison d'être* and constitutes a practice that enables one to find emotional and even spiritual reward. Popular colloquialisms such as "retail therapy" or "treat yo self" reflect and reinforce this psychological trend. Social media-inspired global travel does the same, with extremely deleterious consequences for local communities and ecosystems, as well as the Earth's atmosphere. To be sure, consumption is not inherently bad—we all have to eat, as the saying goes. It is simply that the magnitude of contemporary consumption is so significant and so premised on a carbon economy that consumerism has become a central driver of climate change. Given the thick cultural support for fossil fueled consumerism, the tractability of addressing climate change fades even further into the distance.

There are, of course, other sources of climate wildness. Environmental racism, anthropocentrism, patriarchy, and an exaggerated focus on the present over the future all perpetuate the status quo and thus encourage a blindness to the urgency and profundity of climate change (Detraz, 2017; Gardiner, 2011; Hage, 2017; White, 1967). Moreover, polarizing politics encourage climate skepticism, as populist leaders such as US President Donald Trump and Brazilian President Jair Bolsonaro use climate change denial as a litmus test of political conservativism and loyalty. These, along with other factors, conspire to frustrate collective action on climate protection. Climate wildness, as a result, has become a galloping horse that has thrown off its reins. To be sure, many people are making substantial and even heroic mitigation efforts to stabilize climate. Innovation and investment in renewables, gains in energy efficiency, policy initiatives like the US Green New Deal, and changed individual and collective behavior are trying to recapture the reins. But humanity has inserted its hand too deeply into the Earth's climate system, with a diminishing ability to restrict its reach or to steady the biochemical consequences it has activated. The planet's climate has gone into a tailspin.

Climate Engineering

Humanity has rarely met risk with complacency—something clearly demonstrated by the modern project to banish wildness. In fact, just by themselves, the extraction and use of fossil fuels reflect people's impulse to tame the world around them, as I have been arguing. It is no surprise then that, in the face of runaway climate change, some people are dreaming up ways to exert control over the Earth's atmosphere itself, to avoid the most extreme dangers of climate intensification. Unwilling to live in a warmer world, they see promise in extending human power over the planet's atmospheric infrastructure. Just as wildness was beaten out of people's immediate lives, there is hope of beating it completely out of the Earth's atmospheric conditions. It is as if the long dream of human mastery is finally being challenged at the global level; and a number of thinkers believe humanity is up to the task.

The most dramatic type of atmospheric control comes in the form of geoengineering. Geoengineering involves not stopping carbon and other GHGs emissions but masking or blunting them. It entails deliberately manipulating the planet's physical functionality—the amount of sunlight hitting the Earth or the chemical composition of the atmosphere—in response to anthropogenic climate change. Geoengineers see little hope in humanity's reducing its carbon footprint anytime soon and thus are stepping in as saviors to buy short-term relief or even, theoretically, long-term stability.

Geoengineering, as currently envisioned, comes in two primary varieties. First is solar radiation management (SRM). SRM aims to cool the planet by reflecting incoming sunlight back into space before it can warm the surface of the Earth. SRM proposals include shooting aerosols into the atmosphere to diffuse sunlight, orbiting mirrors to reflect sunlight back into space, and brightening clouds to enhance their reflective properties.

Aerosol injection entails high-flying aircraft releasing reflective participles, such as sulfates, into the upper atmosphere. Sulfates would surround the planet, filter sunlight, and thus serve as a protective shield. Proponents of aerosol injection point out that the Earth itself mimics such action when volcanoes erupt. It is well established that the sulfur dioxide particles emitted by volcanoes do, in fact, block sunlight and have in the past lowered global temperatures. Proponents of SRM suggest that pumping sulfates or other reflective chemicals into the atmosphere is cheap, effective, and almost guaranteed. To be sure, they admit that there are hard to identify side effects and, even more importantly, that chemicals released into the upper atmosphere will eventually dissipate within months, or at most a year, and thus would need to be constantly replenished. Nonetheless, aerosol injection remains one of the most researched options within the suite of geoengineering responses.

The concept of sending orbiting mirrors into space is less developed but works on the same principle. Much like telecommunication satellites, mirrors could be placed into orbit and directly block incoming sunlight. The advantage of such solar deterrents is that they would circle the Earth without the need for constant maintenance or replacement. They could be catapulted into space by rockets and electromagnetic launchers and would avoid some of the side effects associated with aerosol injection, insofar as they would not interact chemically with the Earth's atmosphere. As with sulfate injection, here too there are many unknowns—including how many mirrors would make a discernible difference—but the idea, according to some, holds promise (Gorvett, 2016).

Cloud brightening has received more attention and represents one of the more attractive options since it entails less heavy lifting than either sulfate infusion or orbiting mirrors. Almost all clouds reflect some sunlight. Researchers speculate that, under appropriate conditions, they could seed low-level clouds with sea salt or other compounds to enhance clouds' reflective properties. Most schemes envision a small fleet of ships pumping substances through long tubes that extend 3,000 feet into the air. Like sulfates, such particles would not last long. They might remain in the lower atmosphere for a number of weeks and thus would, like sulfates, have to be constantly reloaded. Like other SRM options, marine cloud brightening represents an attempt to take over the atmosphere—to reengineer it so it works to stave off the most extreme heating. SRM aims to exert control over global wildness by altering the planet's organic infrastructure. If successful, it would, in Naomi Klein's words, replace the sky with a ceiling (2014, p. 224). It would, in other words, push the human "inside" to the far "outside" of earthly limits.

Carbon dioxide removal (CDR) is the second primary form of geoengineering. Like SRM, it aims not to reduce emissions, but to capture CO_2 at the moment of release or after it has entered the atmosphere. Seen by many as the more attractive option, since it entails fewer side effects, CDR is technologically more challenging and lacks a real-world corollary, such as volcanoes, to substantiate its potential. Nonetheless, researchers and political leaders are devoting tremendous effort to bring such schemes on board.

CDR is an umbrella phrase for a suite of efforts. The most promising of these is, arguably, carbon capture and storage (CCS), which, under one scenario, involves trapping carbon within fossil fuel power plants and redirecting into underground cavities. CCS can be used either before or after burning fossil fuels to isolate and absorb CO_2. Once separated from other compounds, CO_2 can be transported to an appropriate storage site. Compressors push CO_2, in liquid or gaseous form, through pipelines. The CO_2 is then stored either underground or underwater. On land, it can be injected into reservoirs that previously held oil and gas. These are usually made of porous rock and thus are capable of holding CO_2 indefinitely. It can also, theoretically, be injected into basalt formations and contained as limestone. Underwater storage is more challenging, since carbon must be released at great depths to ensure that particles fall to the ocean floor rather than return to the surface. The process of CCS rests on the capacity of solvents to separate CO_2 from sulfur, water, and other impurities in the flue gas, pipelines to transport the captured CO_2, and long-term storage options.

CCS aims to remove CO_2 before it enters the atmosphere. If it ever reaches commercial scale, CCS would serve to neutralize the amount of CO_2 being pumped into the air; importantly, it would do nothing to remove already existing carbon concentrations. Direct air capture (DAC), another form of CDR, takes on this latter, more ambitious challenge. It literally pulls CO_2 from ambient air and converts it into calcium carbonate pellets. By heating the pellets, CO_2 can be extracted and then stored in surface canisters. DAC offers itself as a meaningful contribution to addressing climate change since current CO_2 concentrations have already set into motion intensified climate change and, short of reducing them, humanity will have little chance of stabilizing climate. DAC aims to reduce existing CO_2 (Herzog, 2018).

DAC and CDR look so attractive because they do not call on people to stop using fossil fuels but defang the negative consequences of burning them. Combined, they offer the tantalizing promise of "negative emissions." They remove carbon as it is either generated or already present in the atmosphere. Given the profound uncertainties and moral hazard of geoengineering, most advocates look at it as a "Plan B." Geoengineers continually say that mitigation remains the primary strategy for addressing climate change; but, in the absence of strong, international action, geoengineering may be crucial for buying time. It will postpone the worst effects of climate change until humanity can fully commit itself to mitigation. Scientists around the world are acknowledging the need to buy time. The latest IPCC scenarios count on negative emissions to have any chance of staying below 2 degrees Celsius. Without drastic, immediate, worldwide collective action on mitigation, geoengineering increasingly looks necessary.

Climate change is simply another type of wildness and, as such, can in theory be wrestled with and subject to the same approach humanity has always used to confront wildness. SRM and CDR represent a doubling down of human power. They complete the story of extending the indoors out. People turn to fossil fuels to make their lives more comfortable and predictable. In doing so, they unwittingly release so much CO_2 into the atmosphere that the wildness they seek to ban resurfaces at the global level. In the face of this, geoengineers want to expand the scope of humanity's taming abilities. They want to subject the entire globe to human ingenuity and discipline. They see the Earth itself as an object of control—the last frontier of combatting wildness.

We should commend geoengineers for taking the problem seriously. The climate has entered a period of perpetual spasm; it is increasingly volatile, with no sign of calming down. Climate scenarios with more than a two-degree temperature rise represent conditions that researchers are labeling, in terms of sequential heat increases, "unusual," "unfamiliar," and ultimately "unknown" (Frame et al., 2017). This last category captures the essence of wildness. It speaks of a system that is unfolding in nonlinear ways and that exceeds traditional time frames and spatial categories of control. Importantly, even if every nation adheres to its Paris commitment, over half the world would experience an "unknown" climate by 2050, and 80 percent of the world would experience it by 2100 (Frame et al., 2017). Like the hinterlands beyond the first agricultural settlements, climate change represents a phenomenon that is difficult to predict, adapt to, and bring under wraps. In the face of this, geoengineers are recommending the ultimate form of control: to manage the entire planet, to bring the globe itself under human guidance. Geoengineers want to dewild the atmosphere. Should we take the leap? Should our species try to exert mastery over the last frontier?

4

Wild Emptiness

One of the great privileges of affluence is the ability to be alone. It is comforting to close one's door, roll up a car window, or otherwise shut out the world around us. As mentioned, I'm writing this book in my study—a place cordoned off from traffic, weather, and other people. I enjoy relative calm and quiet. I especially love that I can control what goes on in the room. With no one else around and protected from the elements, I can do what I want. I'm king of my experience.

While on the one hand unremarkable, it is nevertheless strange, on the other, that I can be alone. Not only do I share the Earth with over 7.7 billion other people, but I'm a mere grain of sand by comparison with all living creatures on Earth. There are tens of millions of other species and innumerable individual organisms on Earth. They roam the land,

swim in the water, fly through the air, root themselves in the soil. These creatures operate partly on
their own and, in this sense, have their own wildness about them. I am intricately folded into this
wider living world and depend on it to stay alive,
and yet somehow I can largely ignore it as I write
these words and move through my days.

I didn't get here easily. For centuries, humans
domesticated and packaged the world. They learned
how to control other people and nature and thus
created conditions of insular privilege. Much of this
was the result of fossil fuels. I can adjust my study's
temperature, enjoy the protection of concrete walls,
sit in a manufactured chair, and otherwise ignore
the outside because of coal, natural gas, and oil.
My comfort, however, goes beyond fossil fuels. I'm
the beneficiary of centuries—indeed, millennia—of
humans taking charge of the conditions around
them. I'm the recipient of pushing wildness far from
daily life.

During the agricultural revolution, the first
farmers domesticated plants and animals. They
wrested wildness out of cereals such as lentils,
barley, and flax, as well as out of animals such
as sheep, llamas, and goats. They built settlements
and worked to protect themselves from wild animals and the vicissitudes of the elements. Over the

ages, people extended their reach and colonized increasing areas across the Earth. They perfected the ability to control the world around them. This included encroaching upon and converting unbidden landscapes into farms, cities, and suburbs, and penetrating and harvesting forests, estuaries, oceans, and mountains. It has also involved deciphering and manipulating chemical bonds and the genetic building blocks of life. Through it all, humans have become masters over the so-called plant, animal, and microbial "kingdoms." This doesn't mean that humans determine everything that happens—far from it. But, of all species, *Homo sapiens* now reigns supreme. The few animals most people see anymore are bred pets, cattle, poultry, or fish, or birds, squirrels, and other "weedy species" that can live among humans (Meyer, 2006). The plants most of us come into contact with are specifically cultivated to provide food or create pleasant surroundings. For all intents and purposes, indoor spaces have been rid of other creatures and even outdoor spaces have been significantly formatted. Today the privileged live largely immune from most dangers or annoyances posed by plants, animals, and even microbes, and in the aggregate enjoy the power that comes from turning the nonhuman world into an instrument of desire and design. Whether through farming, mining, landscape design, chemical modification, or manufacturing, humans have turned the living world into a stock of resources. They have dewilded the creeping, swimming, flying world around them.

In a parallel fashion, certain groups have long tamed and controlled other people in pursuit of their own security and comfort. As mentioned, when the first farmers domesticated plants and animals, they not only intensified human control over the natural world but also deepened conditions of social hierarchy and domination over other people. This happened as crop surpluses enabled people to assume different social roles—toolmakers, builders, butchers, priests as well as hunters and farmers—and elites asserted authority through an ability to tax and forcibly keep people toiling in the fields. The colonization of plants and animals has its analogue in the domination of other peoples.

Global Biotic Spasm

Like the power to control the world through fossil fuels, the effort to regulate and diminish others' lives may have created havens of safety and solitude, but it has not gotten rid of wildness. It has simply moved it horizontally—into other people's lives—and vertically—to the globe itself. Ecologically, depleting the nonhuman world by pushing wild fauna and flora to the outskirts of human experience ends up shredding the fabric of essential organic reciprocities and interdependencies. It pokes holes in the living connections within food webs, habitats, mutualistic relationships, and essential chemical processes. The result is the unraveling of the planet's biological support system in the form of biodiversity. Today 1 million species are on the brink of extinction. While many of us no longer need to deal with wild animals, pests, or even overgrown weeds, we must now contend with planetary biological decline. Everywhere, the number, diversity, and health of almost all plants, animals, microorganisms, and even ecosystems are declining, and this attenuates and in many cases destroys provisioning services such as pollination, oxygenation, and wastewater cleansing, incapacitates biodiversity hotspots such as wetlands, coral reefs, and critical forests, and represents a biological holocaust of individual creatures with cascading ecological effects. It is as if, in successfully pushing the living, breathing world of other beings out of our immediate lives, we are crippling the very conditions of life itself.

Such dismemberment has become its own type of wildness. Like climate change, humans have activated positive feedback loops that reinforce and accelerate biodiversity loss such that continued unraveling is essentially unstoppable. For instance, when faced with decreased catches, fishers sail deeper into the oceans, harvest premature fish, and further decimate global fisheries. As gorillas, tigers, and elephants grow further endangered, poachers move deeper into forests, hunt with more intensity, and drive such animals closer to extinction. Likewise, as people kill pesky insects through various insecticides or electronic zappers, they remove food for birds, lizards, spiders, and other creatures, and thus intensify the spiraling down of ecological functionality. These processes are well underway and reinforce global biotic spasm.

Biodiversity has to do with the multiplicity of ecosystems, the genetic make-up of individual creatures, and species variation. Biodiversity is important as it provides resilience to disturbance and ensures biological health and longevity. By almost any measure, human action is simplifying ecosystemic, genetic, and species variety. Agricultural monoculture, habitat incursion, pollution, invasive species, deforestation, and climate change are thinning out landscapes and seascapes. These same factors are interfering with the genetic make-up of certain species and thus depriving classes of organisms of chromosomal protection in the face of disease and illness. Finally, they conspire to kill off species themselves. While extinction has always occurred, now it is happening at thousands of times the normal background rate. It is so severe that many say we are living in the equivalent of the planet's sixth great extinction.

Despite significant concerted efforts, the world has yet to cauterize the biological hemorrhaging. More significant than numbers, the dynamics of biodiversity loss signal a process that is out of control and grows more so by the day. A combination of positive feedback loops, ecological complexity, and the full admixing of the human and nonhuman realms—to say nothing of significant economic and political interests that work against biodiversity protection—scramble attempts to understand and take effective, collective action on behalf of ecological exuberance. Yes, states have signed international treaties such as the Convention on Biological Diversity (CBD) and the Convention on International Trade in Endangered Species (CITES) and have agreed to a set of forest protection principles. They have also undertaken significant domestic action to stem biological depletion, for example the Endangered Species Act in the United States, the Habitats Directive within the European Union, and the Wildlife Protection Act in India. Despite such initiatives, rates of diminution and extinction continue to accelerate. It is as if governing bodies were trying to stop a locomotive that has left the station and is gathering speed by throwing pebbles onto the tracks. The continual unraveling of life is inexorable.

Humanity's failed attempts to address biodiversity loss mimic those aimed at protecting the climate. Financial interests, embedded within a capitalist economy, drive the search for resources into remote regions, the conversion of forests into agricultural lands, the expansion of roads, and the increase of waste as corporations and whole societies pursue endless material wealth and economic growth. Indeed, as long as people see, or are made to see, material accumulation as the route to well-being, biological variety will plummet. Capitalism and its present-day materialist expression engender the destruction of the nonhuman world.

Similarly, the tragedy of the commons intensifies this challenge, as states are reluctant to sacrifice their perceived self-interest in the service of global biodiversity. The reason why the world has only a set of principles governing forests, lax compliance with the CBD and CITES, and a stubborn inability to craft far-reaching international treaties focused on biodiversity is partly related to the self-regarding character of the state system and to the geopolitical considerations that follow from this. No state contains biological expression exclusively within its own territory. Migratory animals don't stop at national borders, nor do air, water, shifting soils, or dispersing plants. Biodiversity depends on transnational and global interactions. Locked in their own sovereign mindset and animated by the structural constraints of a Westphalian state system, states watch out mainly for their own territories. Biodiversity is a casualty of international politics.

The world is also failing to confront biodiversity loss for a more philosophical reason. People are able to exploit other living beings, because plants and animals are, simply, not human. Plants and animals fail to communicate through human language, lack political representation, and possess little if any obvious rationality. Humanity has long been anthropocentric. The human being sits at the center of value and everything takes on meaning and worth in relation to human interest. From this perspective, nature must translate itself into human significance or risk being unnoticed, disregarded, or exploited. Through anthropocentric lenses, trees are standing timber, fish are swimming protein, and wild mammals are roaming threats. The same goes for the abiotic world insofar as rivers are sources of water, fossilized life appears as potential energy, and mineral-rich mountains represent deposits to be mined.

Anthropocentrism runs deep in the western ethical tradition. Almost all western ethical schools of thought reserve moral consideration for rational, free, reflective individuals—characteristics associated with human beings. The founding thinkers of consequentialist, duty, and virtue ethics, in particular, restrict ethics to humans, as do many religious traditions. When they focus on how one treats others or conceptualize the good life, the other is another human being and the good life is a human life. Since plants and animals seemingly lack developed rationality, operate without obvious signs of cognition, or reveal little by way of introspective consciousness, ethicists rarely grant them moral consideration. To be sure, within the past fifty years or so, quite a few thinkers have argued for extending moral worth to animals (and some even to plants and whole ecosystems) on the basis of sentience, being "subject of a life," or simply phenomenal existence (Abram, 2012; Kimmerer, 2013; Leopold, 1989; Pollan, 2013; Naess, 1973; Regan, 2004; Wohlleben, 2016). But these voices are outliers. Most people are inherently anthropocentric and thus confine moral worth to fellow humans. Exploitation and even disappearance of nonhuman creatures are not problems per se but simply the consequences of building the world as humans see fit.

Anthropocentrism, along with state sovereignty, capitalism, and lack of political will consolidate and intensify wildness in the form of mass extinction and the widespread impoverishing of the living world. Despite many best efforts, people seem unable to stop planetary biological unraveling. The losses are multiplying, ricocheting off one another, and spiraling out of control. It is as if humanity got what it always wished for, but in spades. It has pushed nonhumans so far out of the way that biological diminishment and disappearance have turned into their own, rapidly unfolding phenomena. Surging depletion is upon us and gathering increasing steam. Editing and controlling the nonhuman world may have been an ancient dream of our species, but success has turned the intention into a nightmare.

Pain of Extractivism

Global biological impoverishment represents the vertical dimension of trying to control other creatures. It denotes the catapulting upwards of wildness. The horizontal dimension comes into focus as we notice the process by which biodiversity loss and biotic simplification unfold on the ground. When ecological bonds break or species and ecosystems come under threat, they do not instantly turn into extinctions or affect global processes. At first and perhaps mostly, they tear at and degrade more local ecological features and, in doing so, take a toll on specific living beings. Pollution, intensive farming, and land conversion in general put pressure on other creatures. They pull out the rug from under various plants and animals, damaging and ultimately destroying habitat. When this happens, living things suffer. They either migrate to more accommodating areas (if such places exist) or soldier through the various assaults. Encroaching human activities often crowd animals within smaller areas, contaminate water sources, reduce food availability, and simply steal the robustness with which regions support rich, diverse life. This is the equivalent of torture. Humans slowly—and, often, not so slowly—create conditions for pain as organisms try to survive in the face of biological assault. Some creatures can migrate; even plants can move. Yet such migration is increasingly more difficult as less land is uninhabited, roads and other structures block migration routes, and the forces driving migration—such as climate change—are happening so quickly that creatures are unable to travel fast enough. Biotic diminishment hurts not simply the Earth in the abstract but the winged, finned, rooted, four-legged, and leafed among us. It affects actual, living beings.

Anthropocentrism might help people turn a deaf ear to the pain they are inflicting on other creatures, but, to mix metaphors, it cannot blind them to the pain fellow humans experience. In many parts of the world people live alongside other creatures and have done so for hundreds and, in some cases, thousands of years. This is especially the case of indigenous people, but it also includes many who live in lightly populated, underdeveloped regions. As expanding into remoter areas becomes profitable or otherwise attractive, these people become casualties. Developers and migrants seeking greater economic opportunity encroach upon and often expropriate these people's land. Like their nonhuman counterparts, the victims are displaced to increasingly marginal or degraded areas, or otherwise suffer the negative effects of intrusion. Dramatic examples include oil exploration and development in tribal lands—such as the Ogoniland in Nigeria, or indigenous regions in Ecuador and Peru. Not only do such operations scare away or decimate wild animals—a

2018 oil pipeline spill in northern Colombia killed over 2,400 animals and damaged over 1,000 species of trees—but they also endanger the lives of local, usually tribal people (Zachos, 2018). Irresponsible oil extraction increases the probability of cancer, miscarriages, and other health problems for local residents and, in cases of river contamination or other acute ecosystem assaults, it despoils key food and livelihood sources, increasing hunger and economic disruption. "I have practically nothing to eat," reports a local resident near the spill in Colombia that contaminated the Magdalena River, "we have lived through the river all our lives" (quoted in Zachos, 2018). Sadly, this kind of pattern continues to repeat itself throughout the world. Whether it is oil production, industrial deforestation, agricultural expansion, or climate change, the breaking of ecological and human bonds extends far and wide. It is another example of displacement. In the process of clearing space for human industry and thus pushing plants and animals aside for development, the harm falls on the least well-off. The horizontal spread of taking greater control over the more-than-human world has direct consequences for the politically marginalized, poor, and otherwise disprivileged.

Another way to think about the horizontal dimension is through the concept of extractivism—

the "mindset and pattern of resource procurement based on removing as much material as possible for as much profit as possible" (Willow, 2018, p. 2). Extractivism almost always involves plundering areas of the politically weak and concentrating the resultant generation of wealth into the hands of the few who live, work, and play far from extraction sites themselves. When certain people appear as less deserving, or when plants and animals are seen as dispensable, they become prime targets for exploitation. One reason people can mine land, chop down trees, contaminate waterways, and hunt animals is that the victims often appear voiceless. Likewise, one reason poor people suffer the indignities of land development, agricultural expansion, and so forth is that they are seen as superfluous to the greater aims being undertaken. To be sure, they often protest and otherwise stand up for their rights in various ways. In fact the poor and the politically marginalized engage in extraordinary acts of resistance at great risk. However, such efforts are often limited by disproportionate power. This accounts for environmental injustice across the world. It is no mistake, for instance, that communities of color are regularly subjected to toxic dumps, chemical industries, and mining operations (Bullard, 2000; Taylor, 2014). They often lack the resources to successfully challenge displacement. Likewise, poor neighborhoods or districts where a majority of people do not speak the national language typically are targeted for similar, environmentally hazardous operations. They, like plants and animals that stand in the way of human endeavors, are victims of extractivism—the taking of resources, including labor, without due compensation.

The horizontal dimension of pushing wildness out of our lives represents the beginnings of "how the world breaks" (Cox and Cox, 2016). At first, individuals suffer (unevenly) the consequences of displacement. As assaults accumulate and larger ecological systems get impacted, the organic fabric of life frays, tears, and eventually dissipates. Harm no longer simply afflicts individuals, communities, or even whole countries but amasses at the global level. The globe's organic systems buckle and fragility takes on a planetary face. Wildness abounds.

To Govern Evolution

What to do? How can people respond to global, biological impoverishment? As mentioned, the world has tried to address it in various ways. Governments have drafted treaties and enacted domestic legislation; nongovernmental organizations have undertaken site-specific projects to protect particular areas; and civil society, as a whole, has sounded the alarm about the dangers of mass extinction. Many of these efforts have involved cordoning off critical ecological hotspots, protecting specific endangered species, and drawing and protecting boundaries between overly exploitative human activities and the well-being of the more-than-human world. Such efforts find their roots in the preservationist movement and work to isolate and safeguard ecologically rich lands and waters. Some of these efforts have, indeed, slowed biotic unraveling in certain places, to a limited degree; but, as a whole, they have not stopped the trend of global biodiversity loss. One reason for this is simply that such efforts are too little, too late. People put the engines of global fraying in place so long ago and at such institutional depth that trying to protect a piece of land here or a given species there, while important for many reasons, makes a mere dent in the problem. A second and perhaps more important reason has to do with the logic of such efforts. They are premised on separating and holding back human activities from the wider sphere of all life—an orientation that is necessarily bound to fail in the Anthropocene.

When conservationists win legal protection of areas in the form of establishing a national park, forest, or monument, not only are their efforts reversible (as different governmental administrations can change policies) and often unenforceable (as poachers often outnumber guards or corporate entities push for lax enforcement), but they are also subject to forces that work outside established boundaries. Increasingly, the greatest threats to wildlife are hotter temperatures, pollution, and land modification that takes place beyond protected areas. People cannot simply clear-cut to the edge of a forest, pump billions of tons of carbon into the atmosphere from urban centers, or overfish the seas without consequences for other spaces. Protected areas can never fully be secure in the Anthropocene, since it is impossible to disaggregate humans and nature and to restrict human actions to demarcated effects. As many are learning, the best hope we have for conservation involves not cordoning off places from human influence but skillfully extending human involvement in the service of ecological well-being. Today the most far-reaching conservation efforts include managing so-called wild areas. This involves breeding and reintroducing species, culling overpopulating herds, beating back invasive species, regulating river flows, and fertilizing vegetation. Such tools of the trade are not about getting humans out of the conservation areas but including them in productive ways—ways that benefit both protected regions and the economic livelihoods of local people. While such techniques are useful and demonstrate respect for the complications of sustaining wildlife, sadly, they are far from sufficient. They can influence only so much and, as such, fail to stem the larger biocide.

Enter the technologists. In an attempt to provide a more promising approach, some thinkers acknowledge the impossibility of stopping biodiversity loss and suggest instead selectively repopulating creatures once they go extinct. They imagine taking the reins of species procreation fully into human hands and becoming governors of evolution. The problem with current conservation methods, according to this line of thinking, is that humans have exerted insufficient power over the dynamics of biodiversity. They have gone only partway down the road of active conservation but, to be successful, you must go all the way. This means that, instead of leaving evolution to chance, people must deliberately influence how species come into being. They must take the reins of so-called natural selection. The most dramatic instance of such effort is "de-extinction"— a process by which scientists bring back defunct species. Associated with what is called "resurrection" or "revivalist" science, de-extinction refuses to watch helplessly as the biotic world unravels. Instead, it aims to reweave the threads of genetic, species, and even ecosystem connections (Minteer, 2018; Shapiro, 2015).

Like geoengineering, de-extinction is still in the research phase but certain lines of development are coming into focus. One trajectory involves cloning, whereby genetic material from extinct organisms is used to grow living quasi-replicas. In a number of revealing attempts, scientists are recovering cell nuclei from extinct organisms and placing them into the eggs of living relatives. In one of the most famous efforts, Australian researchers successfully inserted cell nuclei from a frozen specimen of the extinct gastric brooding frog into the eggs of the great barred frog. The eggs turned into living embryos and, although they died three days later, established the technique of reintroducing lost species. The aim is eventually to insert grown embryos into a relative that acts as the host. Called the Lazarus Project, the effort demonstrated the promise of bringing organisms back from the dead (O'Connor, 2015).

Currently researchers are studying how to use the technique to bring back a whole host of extinct species—everything from the passenger pigeon to the woolly mammoth. They are being assisted by the rapid development of genetic technologies. The CRISPR, for instance, is a type of "scissors" that can edit genes with precision. Scientists are developing it for diagnostic purposes and hope ultimately to use it for treating genetic causes of human disease. De-extinctionists plan to use CRISPR to transform the genetic make-up of existing species so they more closely resemble their extinct relatives. The hope is that this will enable more successful cross-breeding. CRISPR will also allow scientists to work with degraded tissue from extinct specimens, and this would greatly expand the menu of possible recoverable species. CRISPR is only one among a host of emerging genetic technologies. Many anticipate that they will greatly accelerate the practice of de-extinction. As environmental scientist Tim Flannery reports in a review of the de-extinction literature, "[t]here is no doubt that we humans have now crossed a technological Rubicon, and at some time in the future extinct species will once again be breathing and interacting with other living things" (Flannery, 2017).

The idea behind de-extinction is not to stop the disappearance of certain plants and animals, or even restrict those activities that drive biotic unraveling. Rather the project aims to replace those vanishing organisms that happen to be on the wrong side of human development. In this sense, de-extinction is, possibly, the ultimate expression of human control. It entails manufacturing species and, importantly, those that humans prefer. The "wild" animals produced would be encoded with human instructions of how to grow and mature and would fit into existing ecosystems only in ways imagined by human beings. De-extinction would completely beat the wildness out of evolution. In the face of biodiversity loss, it would double down on the human impulse to manipulate and shape the world around us. It would extend to the global level the effort that worked to dominate wildness at the local level—the effort to organize and, in the extreme, rid people of the hassle and dangers of plants and animals operating on their own. De-extinction would make humans gods: people would be in control of how life emerges and ultimately which organisms exist.

In the Anthropocene, humans have already become, unintentionally, the governors of evolution in higher vertebrae. De-extinction calls for taking this a significant step further. It entails deliberately overtaking the evolutionary process and becoming conscious authors of the planet's biological future. To be sure, de-extinctionists see themselves acting with their backs against the wall. They are responding to massive anthropogenic extinction and, like their geoengineering counterparts, are crafting a "plan B." In doing so, de-extinctionists aim, paradoxically, to dewild the evolutionary process—to identify, manipulate, and direct its dynamics in particular directions. Should we follow their path? Can and should we control the unfolding of what, until now, has been a human-influenced but still largely self-willing process? Should we become masters of evolution?

5

Rewilding

It seems the height of hubris to ponder master-
ing the Earth. It assumes not only that people can
grab the reins of evolution and climate and steer
them in the direction of their choosing, but that
they have the guts even to try. De-extinction and
geoengineering engage the biophysical workings of
the Earth. They aim to take over evolution and
the composition of the atmosphere. They seek, in
other words, to hack the planet's infrastructure. Is
it wise to be so ambitious? Do we really have it
in us to extend our controlling reach to the edges
of the globe? Isn't this taking the banishment of
wildness too far? These are critically important
questions—but perhaps, at this late date, moot.
Given humanity's long history of conquering wildness, it is hard to imagine not trying to tame the
globe as it spirals out of control. For millennia,

humans have been carving out increasing domains of influence and, in all likelihood, de-extinctionists and geoengineers will continue in that spirit. The momentum is simply too strong. Brave new wildness will, inevitably, face brave new engineering. Choice is probably not a possibility.

Yet choice is exactly what is needed. Humans can no longer afford falling into the future. Engaging wildness with a conquering spirit is precisely what created unstoppable extinction, accelerating climate change, and other disassembling threats in the first place; it is doubtful that it can reverse them. Although challenging, there are other options. Instead of doubling down on control, global spasm invites a rethinking of humanity's relationship with wildness. It offers the chance finally to stop battling the unbidden and unfamiliar and, instead, question what other qualities wildness may require of us. Indeed, brave new wildness creates the imperative to reflect fundamentally on how humans deal with that which eludes control.

Inextinguishable Wildness

Planetary control appears hubristic because it can never entirely work. Despite grandiose designs and a seeming willingness to go global, snuffing out wildness is impossible. Wildness has a way of avoiding capture. As it gets cornered, it moves. This won't change simply because humans are attacking it at the global level. Wildness will not cower as people put human fingers on the Earth's thermostat, or try to direct evolution, or otherwise work to control the planet.

Signs of wildness' stubbornness are evident in the very technologies people are proposing to use. For instance, there is little question that solar radiation management (SRM) can dim the amount of sunlight hitting the planet. However, there are grave uncertainties about regional impacts, military uses, and implementation commitments. For instance, some scenarios suggest that, if SRM were deployed on a very large scale—to offset all the warming from elevated greenhouse gas (GHG) concentrations—Indian and African monsoons might be weakened (Moreno-Cruz et al., 2012). This would potentially impact agriculture that sustains billions of people. Additionally, in the absence of SRM governance, there is nothing to stop nations from using the technology for weather-altering military purposes. Conceivably states, or even non-state actors, could weaponize SRM as a tool of conflict (Macnaghten and Szerszynski, 2013). Finally, because sulfates are short-lived in the atmosphere, the world would have to commit to frequent and almost indefinite injections. At stake is a "termination shock" wherein, in the absence of relentless mitigation, cessation would result in dramatic warming (Jones et al., 2013). Such unknowns and high risks underline that SRM will not rid the world of climate wildness; it simply wagers against it.

Carbon dioxide removal (CDR) possesses similar hazards. There are definitely ways to capture CO_2 from smokestacks (carbon capture and storage, CCS) and even, theoretically, from ambient air (direct air capture, DAC). But significant challenges revolve around what to do with the isolated carbon. Best case scenarios envision injecting it into deep underground cavities or at the bottom of oceans. (Fossil fuel companies imagine using pressurized carbon dioxide to push untapped oil and natural gas deposits to the surface.) The problem is that capturing and transporting CO_2 takes significant amounts of energy, and this creates a vicious cycle of burning additional carbon to remove CO_2— all of which would limit CDR's effectiveness. By some estimates, up to 40 percent of a power plant's production would go to capturing and transporting carbon (Rochon, 2008). No reliable estimates measure energy costs for DAC. More troubling is figuring out how to keep the deposited carbon underground or on the ocean floor. Models suggest that porous rock could contain significant pressure and certain geological cavities are essentially air-tight. This is especially the case with emptied oil and gas reservoirs that held deposits previously over geologic time. Models also suggest that CO_2 injected at great ocean depths would fall rather than rise to the surface. But, even in ideal conditions, there is no safeguard against leakage and escape. And, if deposited carbon eventually makes its way back into the atmosphere, not only does the entire effort become worthless but the additional and unanticipated CO_2 would heat the planet that much more.

The most daunting challenge of CDR involves scaling up operations to make a significant difference. Currently, there are only a handful of facilities throughout the world using or experimenting with CCS and, given the countless number of power stations, steel mills, cement plants, and other point sources, CCS has a long way to go before it would be commercially viable and have a significant impact on carbon emissions. The same goes especially for DAC. Companies like Carbon Engineering, Global Thermostat, and Climeworks are currently able to remove roughly 140 tons of CO_2 per day or just over 51,000 tons per year (National Academies of

Sciences, Engineering, and Medicine, 2018). This pales in the face of the thirty-six billion tons that are emitted each day and of the even greater amount that already saturates the atmosphere (ibid.).

Similar risks and challenges accompany de-extinction. Huge complexities plague the challenge of genetically creating viable species and approximating extinct creatures. In theory, splicing genetic sequences is certainly possible and rudimentary experiments show promise. However, perfecting the process to the point where people can confidently design viable new life-forms is far from certain. Great complexities revolve around isolating, removing, and transplanting individual genes from one species to another. The margin of error is narrow and thus results are hard to control. Additional challenges will arise as researchers insert extinct relatives into existing ecosystems. Air, water, soil, flora, fauna, and microbial life have changed dramatically since the woolly mammoth or aurochs walked the Earth. How such creatures would survive and interact with existing ecological conditions is anyone's guess. Reintroduced creatures will arrive as exotic species with perhaps no known predators; moreover, their mere existence may upset food chains and ecological interdependencies. They may, in other words, launch a global Jurassic Park. Far from stemming biodiversity loss, de-extinction may actually fuel it. It would not clamp down on the wildness of cascading extinction but intensify it.

A different kind of wildness revolves around what economists call moral hazard. If people think that extinct species can be reengineered and reintroduced, they may not worry or take steps to prevent biodiversity loss. They could continue overhunting, encroaching on habitat, and otherwise wiping out plants and animals, in the belief that humans can simply bring back what is lost. Similarly, if people see geoengineering as a panacea for climate change, they may refrain from mitigation and thus never genuinely address the problem. This is especially troubling with sulfate injection SRM because, as mentioned, once one stops releasing particles to block sunlight, temperatures will rise dramatically, as built-up CO_2 traps that much more heat. This form of social wildness may not be as obvious as ecological ones, but it nevertheless introduces significant uncertainty, unpredictability, and extreme danger.

Everything, of course, has risks, so fear that things may not go as planned does not itself disqualify geo-technologies. What it does do, however, is underscore the quixotic effort to control evolution and the planet's carbon cycle. There will never be a time when humans master the more-than-human world or even themselves. As political theorist Hannah Arendt (1998) points out, human action constantly introduces novelty to the world. Like birth itself, it interjects unpredictability. Furthermore, as any biologist will attest, it is impossible to calculate the unfolding of ecosystem dynamics. There are simply too many interacting factors in a changing set of conditions. Humans may have done a miraculous job of circumscribing wildness in their immediate lives. But, as wildness takes on a global face, the limits of such effort become more obvious. Cranking down on unpredictability at the global level, like trying to rid it anywhere, is a game of whack-a-mole. The more one pushes, the more wildness scatters. The problem this time is that, in its accumulative and condensed form, global wildness wagers with planetary well-being.

Rewilding

One can imagine a different approach. Although it may sound blasphemous, what if we gave up the dream of mastery? What if we held on to ingenuity and feats of engineering, but placed them in a humbler context instead of being deluded by visions of planetary discipline? For too long, people have identified sources of danger and discomfort outside themselves and have thus worked to control the world around them. This is what was behind the most aggressive efforts during the agricultural revolution and the modern period, and now it informs geoengineering and de-extinction efforts. But what if humans ceased to look outside for the source of their troubles? What if they relinquished the impulse to remake the world in their own image? Confronting global wildness offers that opportunity. It provides a chance to rethink how humans relate to wildness in general. The globe is not simply the next frontier of wildness to be conquered but represents the folly of the entire dominating project.

Instead of dewilding the world, what if we did the opposite? Rather than define unruliness as the enemy and keep pushing it out of human experience, what if we welcomed more of it? What if we accepted that which eludes control, rather than bracing against it? What if, in other words, we were to *rewild* ourselves and our the world?

Rewilding means different things to different people. For some, it involves releasing captive animals back into the wild. For others, it entails reintroducing species to areas where they previously roamed or restoring ecosystems to a time when humans exerted only minimal pressure and influence. For others still, it means creating historically new "conditions for nature to take care of itself" and proceed largely by its own design (Tanasescu, 2017, p. 334). All these orientations share the view of George Monbiot, an environmental journalist who defines rewilding as "resisting the urge to control nature and allowing it to find its own way" (2015, p. 9).

In the Anthropocene, of course, it is impossible for nature to "find its own way." Humans have imprinted themselves too deeply into every ecosystem. There is no place anymore where nature exists in a pristine form; there is no spot devoid of a human signature. If nothing else, climate change itself obliterates the line between nature and humans. But rewilding is not about seeking an unadulterated future for what we generally call nature; it is simply about creating more space for other beings and processes. It involves taking the human foot off the conquering gas pedal. As such, it offers an orientation or even a quality to be cultivated rather than a set of requirements that demand orthodox observance.

Conservation biologists have been pursuing a particular variant of rewilding for a few decades now. They focus on wildlife and seek its well-being by establishing so-called cores, corridors, and carnivores (Foreman, 2004). Cores are areas large enough for animals to hunt and forage, move seasonally, and have their day-to-day needs met. They are places of sustained habitation and consist usually of protected parks, forests, and wilderness areas. Since most core areas are too small to maintain animal populations over the long term, conservation biologists also recommend building corridors to connect cores. Corridors guard against geographic isolation and allow wildlife to traverse cities, towns, and agricultural areas. Today the European green belt provides relief for wildlife from Finland to Greece; Banff wildlife bridges enable animals to traverse highways and fragmenting roads in British Columbia, Canada; and the Terai Arc Landscape links eleven protected areas in India and Nepal. Cores and corridors supply the infrastructure for rewilding by sustaining large carnivores. Carnivores are critical in that they create and maintain structure, resilience, and diversity in ecosystems by acting as top predators and ensuring healthy trophic interactions. They provide the electricity that invigorates ecosystems. Taken together, these three ingredients provide a strategy for rewilding. They support the possibility of letting nature take a bit more of its own course.

Rewilding is not simply a vision and tool of conservation. As a general orientation, it sees the unknown and the other not as threats but as things to come to terms with, and even to value and appreciate. It recommends holding back the controlling human hand and, instead of imposing ourselves on the unfamiliar and unwieldy, finding ways of opening to them. This means accepting and even inviting a certain amount of wildness into our lives.

Rewilding, in this more general sense, provides guidance for climate change and biodiversity loss. One reason why people continue to burn immense amounts of fossil fuels is that they seek not only security but also the comfort and convenience that cheap, available energy provides. This includes, for instance, the convenience of driving private cars instead of walking or taking public transit, eating food from around the world independently of the time of year, keeping indoor temperatures steady regardless of season, and buying an endless supply of consumer goods for every fancy. It also includes the convenience of governments subsidizing fossil fuels to appease industry and to keep consumer energy prices low, and the convenience corporations sell in the form of labor-saving devices or simply entertainment. There is, of course, nothing wrong with convenience per se. The world has abundant resources to meet people's needs and much else. Moreover, it makes sense that people have an aversion to discomfort. But the push for convenience at all costs, through profligate fossil fuel use, registers its cost in atmospheric carbon.

Rewilding calls for rethinking convenience. At the individual level, this means resisting the move to turn an ignition key, flip a switch, purchase another unneeded item, or otherwise act impulsively to satisfy every retail itch. It means, in other words, coming out of one's comfort zone. This may include putting oneself at the mercy of public transit, interacting with more strangers, eating more local and seasonal foods, and feeling colder in the winter and hotter in the summer. It may involve turning out more lights, taking fewer and shorter showers, refusing to travel to every gathering, and reducing one's energy use overall. It also includes rejecting single-use items, retrofitting one's home and business with solar energy, and lobbying government officials to enact climate protection legislations. In all of this, the ease of life will take a hit. People will have less freedom and will have to confront more vulnerability. They will have to expend more time in the service of civic duty. In these circumstances life will grow wilder. At the same time, however, the globe will grow a bit less wild. Reducing humanity's carbon footprint serves as a relief valve on global wildness.

Rewilding

Something similar has to happen at the collective level. Economic growth is important but irrelevant on a reeling and dying planet. Moreover, there are ways to sustain economies without stripping the world of resources and shooting fossil fueled waste into the sky. Rewilding, in this context, requires transitioning to clean energy. This means putting a price on carbon, investing in solar, wind, and hydroelectric power, and pursuing dramatic infrastructure efficiencies. It includes fostering a culture beyond consumerism and directing technological progress toward sustained mitigation. Such policy measures may sound simply like more managerial control—a type of cranking down on human behavior. They are different, however, as they require significant costs, tack into unknown waters, and focus attention toward a shift in human behavior rather than human control over increasingly far-flung earthly realms. Transitioning to a renewable economy involves phasing out certain jobs and perhaps whole industries, investing in new forms of infrastructure, and reorganizing economic and political power. It requires developing ways to store intermittent sources of energy and, short of this, using less energy. There are many unknowns and potential dislocations associated with mitigating climate change, and thus there is bound to be much discomfort. This is why people have generally failed in mitigation efforts. There is some wildness involved. But inviting that wildness into our collective lives is essential if it means defusing global climate intensification.

Rewilding takes on the same character regarding biodiversity loss. As mentioned, 1 million plant and animal species are on the verge of extinction. Many factors drive this—for example, growing population numbers, capitalist imperatives, and cultural understandings that belittle the lives of other creatures and encourage overharvesting, pollution, and deforestation. But these are active within a wider orientation of securing greater comfort and convenience. For instance, farmers and agrobusinesses cut down forests in search of cheaper land and less expensive crop production. Urban developers do the same as they seek larger tracts of real estate and peddle the promise of suburban living. Corporate fleets and even individuals overharvest fish and timber to save money and avoid more challenging methods of resource capture. Likewise, mining companies denude landscapes (often harming indigenous communities) to profit from untapped oil, coal, or other minerals and to cut corners on extraction. Convenience also drives farmers to overuse pesticides and antibiotics and manufacturers to release pollutants into air, water, and soil. Rewilding demands putting an end to such short-sighted, convenience-oriented practices. It requires assuming the hardship of facing up to the full ecological costs of doing business. It involves individually and collectively pulling back and reducing humanity's bootprint on the more-than-human world.

Establishing cores and corridors and reintroducing carnivores goes part of the way toward doing this. It offers the promise of enhancing biological abundance, diversity, and resilience. But this is far from enough. People need to accept the inconvenience and hardship that come from caring about the lives of other creatures. Reintroduced wolves *will* eat cattle; setting up wildlife corridors *will* endanger people as predatory animals roam closer to humans; farming without pesticides *will* cost more; limiting fishing *will* lead to job losses and industry adjustment; containing agricultural and urban expansion *will* create pressure to use land more efficiently. Moreover, corporate actors must themselves reflect critically on their seeming need to push for endless market share, power accumulation, and control; and governments and civil society must put in place corporate constraints. All this will be a challenge and will invite discomfort; it will also involve looking inside ourselves and asking what we are capable of and what kinds of changes we wish to take on and inhabit. As such, it flirts with more wildness. But this might be an attractive trade-off, especially as it is seen in the context of cascading biological decline. Rewilding can release some of the pressure that sends species to extinction and diminishes ecological well-being. It reverses the push upward and redistributes wildness.

Of course, none of this is new. For decades, environmentalists have been pleading to reduce humanity's ecological footprint, make more room for other beings, and live in sustainable ways. Sustainability means recognizing limits and living within the planet's ecological means. Unresponsive to such warnings, humans have continued to engage in a war against anything that frustrates their intentions, anything that operates to its own beat. The results of doing so have finally come to roost in the form of planetary fragility. The Earth itself has become compromised through the pursuit of more comfortable lives. It is time to take another path.

Care and Thriving on a Diminished Earth

Rewilding speaks not simply to the vertical dimension of brave new wildness but also the horizontal one. As author Mark Bekoff (2014) explains, rewilding involves building not simply physical pathways between protected areas but interpersonal ones between people. Bekoff suggests a rewilding of the heart wherein people create corridors of compassion and coexistence not only with plants and animals but also with fellow human beings. Rewilding, in this sense, includes opening more to the needs and challenges that others face and pursuing greater justice. This invites more wildness as it destabilizes privilege and, out of respect for others, denies the satisfaction of every desire.

Geoscientists tell us that we live in the Anthropocene—the "age of humans." This is a misnomer. Today a handful of individuals and states are responsible for the bulk of environmental degradation. For instance, with less than 5 percent of the world's population, the United States nevertheless consumes over "one-third of the world's paper, a quarter of the world's oil, 23 percent of the coal, 27 percent of the aluminum, and 19 percent of the copper" ("Use It and Lose It," 2002), and a mere hundred companies account for 70 percent of greenhouse gases (Griffin, 2017). Such disproportion is especially galling as those who consume and emit the least suffer the most from humanity's impact. This suggests that the Anthropocene should be more

accurately defined as the "age of *some* humans."
Some of us—the powerful, wealthy, and otherwise
privileged (of which I consider myself a part)—are
more responsible for wrecking the planet's organic
infrastructure than others. We may do so unintentionally; as resource-rich participants in a capitalist
economy and globalized consumerist culture driven
by corporate interests, it is often hard to do otherwise. Rewilding demands taking on the hardship of
change. It requires extricating ourselves as much as
possible from environmental and social exploitation or extractivist mindsets and practices. It takes
seriously environmental injustice and tries to tread
lightly on others as well as on the land, and this
has significant costs. For instance, we can no longer
dump waste on or wrest resources from other communities without transparency, consent, and fair
compensation. We can no longer live off sacrifice
areas such as global free trade zones, which rely on
exploitative labor practices so the rest of us can buy
cheaper products and live at a distance from pollut-
ing industries. We can no longer ignore the coming
plight of future generations either. Future generations are, arguably, the most vulnerable because
they lack political voice and representation and
yet face the greatest threats from intensifying climate change and biological unraveling. Rewilding

involves taking their interests to heart and acting, even in costly ways, to ensure a livable future. None of this will be easy. Seeking justice *is* inconvenient. It takes not only time but material and psychological sacrifice and invites more uncertainty and less control. But that is the price for retracting the wildness that the privileged have long flooded into the other people's lives and are thrusting into the lives of future generations.

The payoff of rewilding is not simply a matter of justice or prudent protection from global catastrophe. As the long tradition of preservationist thinking demonstrates, it also offers an opportunity to feel more alive. This is certainly what people like Henry David Thoreau (1992), John Muir (2011), Aldo Leopold (1989), Robin Kimmerer (2013) and David Abram (2011) have proclaimed. Being exposed to the elements, feeling one's animality, experiencing vulnerability in the face of mystery, and simply encountering wildness is not strictly a burden but can be a rush. It can enliven life. This is why many lamented the closing of the American frontier and continue to complain about reducing protected areas and taming all elements of life. Many feel that there is a part of themselves that thrives in the face of the unbidden, feral, and unpredictable. They recoil when stuck inside houses, cars, and workplaces, constantly among people, and forced to see the human signature everywhere. They wince at too much comfort. While most of humanity has worked to enlarge the "inside," dissident voices throughout the ages have feared what happens when the inside grows too overwhelming. Rewilding extends the invitation to cultivate a sense of wonder and exhilaration in the face of unpredictability. It thus serves both as a response to Earth-rattling climate change and mass extinction and as an embrace of a broader sense of one's humanity.

6

Wild Ethics

Rewilding may sound like a mere adjustment. People will be a little colder here, have less energy there; they will need to take a bus rather than a car; they will have to organize politically. This suggests that we need only sacrifice and invite a bit of uncertainty into our lives and all will be well. Not true; not even close. Rewilding attempts to release wildness out of the global system and out of the lives of the less fortunate; but, short of wholesale societal transformation, such relief will be far from enough. Rewilding, like geoengineering and de-extinction, is no silver bullet. At its best, it will merely dampen the most extreme consequences of climate change and biodiversity loss. While this is nothing to scoff at and, in fact, represents a noble and important goal, it will not release enough global wildness to ward off dramatic, planetary, ecological decline or ameliorate the injustices that accompany environmental intensification. It will not, as many hope, "save the planet." But, that's not the point—or, at least, not the whole point. As mentioned, rewilding is a *response* to global spasm; it is not an answer. There is no answer.

The Earth is presently going through the opening portal of immense, unprecedented environmental disruption. Climate change and biodiversity loss have come to symbolize the portal, but they alone don't define it. Freshwater scarcity, widespread toxification, soil erosion, deforestation, desertification, and a host of other environmental dilemmas collectively and synergistically pose catastrophic threats to the future of life. Sadly, it is too late to nip any of these in the bud and, as should be clear, their cumulative effect is beyond a commanding grasp. Indeed, the most vulnerable people are already experiencing environmental hardship. This is a given. Soon, everyone will feel the pain. To be sure, we can still blunt the hurt, and this is essential. But there are no escape hatches. "Horizontal" and "vertical" wilding are upon us.

Humanity has faced severe challenges in the past. It has been wracked by world wars, extreme famines, rampant disease, immiserating poverty, grinding exploitation. Global wildness, however, represents something new. It's sheer scale and ferocity are unprecedented. Never in human history has the Earth's infrastructure been thoroughly compromised. Never before in humanity's tenure has planetary homeostasis been in doubt. The Anthropocene, to say it plainly, spells ecocide. Humans are unraveling the biophysical conditions of life. They have sent the planet into convulsion. This is not a matter of local, regional, national, or even international shuddering; it is global paroxysm. By throwing wildness out of their immediate lives, people have opened the equivalent of Earth's Pandora's box. As ethicist Clive Hamilton (2017, p. 43) puts it, the slumbering "giant has been awakened"; "Gaia has been enraged." Planetary dismemberment has begun.

Brave new wildness is not simply a matter of scale and intensity but also a matter of quality. When local wildness gets pushed upward and outward, it grows into an entirely different entity; it takes on a fundamentally new character. Until recently, when people pushed unpredictability out of their lives, they *encountered* wildness. They came upon something at the edge of experience, something outside themselves, that threatened or inconvenienced them. Whether it was seasons, darkness, other cultures, or hinterlands beyond human settlements, wildness stood as an exterior challenge to design and control. It represented something beyond one's grasp that had its own agency and dynamic. In contrast, the wildness of climate change, mass extinction, and freshwater scarcity is not *beyond* our grasp but is the planetary expression *of* our grasp. The hand that, in earlier times, pushed away unpredictability has become wildness itself. It shakes through the atmosphere, land, and oceans as well as the interstices of evolution. No longer is wildness the other; it is, rather, humanity itself gone global. Insecurity and discomfort no longer emerge at the edge of control but are themselves consequences of control. Humanity has brought wildness fully *inside*.

Rewilding, while not a solution, represents an approach that takes seriously the scale and character of brave new wildness. It calls on us to stop feeling annoyed, threatened, and endangered by everything that escapes control and to resist the urge constantly to direct and dominate the world around us. Wildness is not an enemy but a fact of life. To be sure, we can and must continue to manage risk and avoid deliberately putting ourselves in harm's way. But coping with risk doesn't mean getting rid of it; and every uncertainty doesn't represent harm. This is especially the case as humans have become authors of much danger and insecurity. Rewilding encourages us to cease battling the unknown and unwieldy and to cultivate a new relationship with them. It calls for accepting wildness and seeing what human life can be like with such accommodation.

Moral Engagement

Befriending wildness doesn't mean throwing in the towel when it comes to climate change, mass extinction, or any other environmental challenge. Accommodation doesn't equal resignation. It means engagement, but of a certain kind. Befriending involves an attitude shift. Instead of a technocratic view that sees every challenge as a puzzle in need of a solution, accommodation encourages ethical sensitivity and commitment. It invites people to care more about how they treat each other and nature than about how they might solve a given dilemma. This shift is essential since global wildness, at its deepest, is not a losing battle—wherein humans fail to pin down global spasm—but a moral challenge.

One reason the Earth is warming and species are disappearing is that modern life deafens many to the plight of others. People mine fossil fuels with little regard for local communities and spew carbon into the atmosphere unaware or unconcerned that the most vulnerable and future generations will suffer disproportionately. Likewise, they cut down forests and otherwise expand into remote areas with little knowledge of or regard for local people or other creatures' habitats. They are able to do all this partly because the moral costs of action are lost in long commodity chains, the complexities of simply doing business, or the abstraction of small, local actions having distant, cumulative effects. Nonetheless, the result is the same. *People throw environmental harm onto the lives of others rather than deal with it themselves.* They toss it across space, time, and species. They send it to other communities, the future, and into the lives of other creatures. In each case, some benefit while others suffer. Too many ignore those on the receiving end. They turn a deaf ear to the vulnerable and politically weak, whether human or nonhuman. In this sense, climate change and mass extinction represent more than technical problems. They are atmospheric and terrestrial expressions of injustice. As such, they demand an ethical response.

Global wildness also calls for an ethical response in a more existential sense. It confronts us with the question of the kind of people we want to be as we travel through the portal of environmental intensification. Many occupy themselves with wondering whether humanity will "make it." They want to know whether the human species will survive. The environmental writer Bill McKibben asks about this as he ponders the strong possibility of humans "faltering." He genuinely wonders whether the human game has played itself out. "Put simply," he writes, "between ecological destruction and technological hubris, the human experience is now in question" (McKibben, 2019, p. 1.) Charles Mann raises similar doubts as he notes that all successful species go extinct and that *Homo sapiens* appears to be spectacularly successful. Like other triumphant species, humans have taken advantage of abundant food and resources but, after growing in number and consumptive size and building institutions premised on plunder, they are outstripping conditions of support and face potential die-off (Mann, 2014). Wallace-Wells (2019), Elizabeth Kolbert (2014), and other observers share a similar view. They look at the scientific evidence and conclude that there is no way the human species—or at least large chunks of it—will survive severe environmental decline.

A more immediate question, however, has to do less with "making it" and more with living together. Global wildness is upon us; we are in the portal. How will we comport ourselves as the world unravels? How will we treat one another in the midst of marshaling individual and collective effort to address climate change, biodiversity, ozone depletion, and the rest? There is a real possibility that, as things get worse, humans will display the nastiest parts of themselves. This would create an increasingly merciless, cut-throat world wherein people fight over scarce resources, struggle to insulate themselves from the fate of others, and self-interestedly protect themselves at the expense of others. This may include authoritarian figures employing ways to weather the ecological storm that divide rather than unite and entail violence rather than collective effort. Alternatively, one can imagine a more cooperative situation, wherein people care about one another, pursue a common fate, and commit to mutual aid. One can imagine building resilience to global wildness—a resilience that fundamentally enhances human dignity and deepens democratic decision-making. This kind of response aims to build our common humanity in the act of responding to global spasm. The ethical sensibility associated with rewilding aims for this latter image. It focuses less on the endgame and more on the quality of ethical life at this unique historical moment. It asks about moral obligations, virtues, and responsibilities.

Coming Home

The war against wildness is fundamentally about extractivism. It involves drilling, fishing, mining, harvesting, enslaving, hollowing out, and otherwise using other people, creatures, or the Earth itself. Extractivism is different from consumption in that, while every living thing needs to eat and use resources to survive, extractivism assumes little agency in other people or organisms and solely appropriates, without compensation or replacement. Extractivism takes minerals, uses people, and enslaves animals without returning anything to them in exchange. It is a one-way interaction (Klein, 2014, p. 169). Rewilding requires adopting a more reciprocal relationship. Instead of expropriation, it offers mutuality; instead of exploitation, partnership; instead of seizing, sharing; instead of depletion, sustaining. Sometimes this translates into entitlements and equal treatment. The Environmental Justice and Animal Liberation movements often use a language of rights to fight extractivism. Other times it demands simply due consideration. Other people, animals, plants, and even ecosystems have a dimension of subjectivity or interiority about them. If they are living, they have an interest in self-preservation and the avoidance of pain; if not, they deserve at least thoughtfulness, since humans share the Earth with them. When we open ourselves to wildness, when we stop fighting and invite more of it into our lives, we extend moral consideration to these other beings and realms. We show sensitivity and practice an element of redress. We see them not as enemies or mere objects of exploitation but rather as fellow humans, kin creatures, intrinsically valuable beings, and life-supporting ecosystems. This doesn't mean that humans stop consuming, but that they treat subjects of consumption with respect. They treat them not merely as means to personal ends, but partly as ends in themselves. Rewilding necessitates developing a less extractivist orientation to the world around us.

Rewilding also casts a discerning eye toward the purpose of much human action. People have long pushed wildness outward in search of security and convenience. They have defined safety and comfort in terms of banishing the unknown and controlling the world around them; and they have sought these at all costs. But are these the most meaningful of goals, and are we defining them accurately? While security is essential for making anything in life possible, there is a fine line between it and comfort and convenience. Rewilding demands scrutinizing the distinction and asking whether ease and expediency are worthy of humanity's profoundest dedication. Global wildness confronts us with an existential challenge. To face it holding fast to comfort as the guiding principle devalues and arguably misunderstands the depth of the challenge and of human life. It blocks access to ethical values beyond simple ease. It occludes the cultivation of virtues such as compassion, courage, and human excellence, which have long informed the ethical tradition (Bringhurst and Zwicky, 2018).

Rewilding offers a further principle for ethically living in the portal of environmental intensification, namely healing the divide between ourselves and the world around us. For millennia, humans have worked to wrench themselves from nature and to distinguish their kin or social group from humanity as a whole. This is what the whole effort to battle wildness has been about. It has rested on a dichotomy between humans and nature and between some humans and others, and implicitly imposes hierarchy and conflict. This has placed struggle at the root of human experience. It basically suggests that life is a clash between me and the world—between the self and everything else. This ignores both biological and social reality. Humans are themselves made of millions of other organisms. In our eyelids, across our skin, and throughout our gut, we are made of an almost infinite number of other organisms. Moreover, every day we depend on other creatures to feed and delight us and absorb our waste. This also goes in the other direction. In many instances, other creatures depend on humans to sustain their lives. This is especially the case in the Anthropocene but has been going on for a long time, as farmers, ranchers, and conservationists have worked to enhance soil fertility, biodiversity, and ecological protection. The same is true socially. No one can make it on their own. We were all born of mothers and depended on them and on others to biologically sustain us during our first months; and we all rely on social networks and collective infrastructure simply to get through our days. It has always been this way. Distinguishing and extricating ourselves from these webs and practicing extractivism makes a mockery of our embeddedness and fundamentally misunderstands the human condition. Moreover, it speaks of moral blindness, as we feel no obligation to treat the world of which we are a part with deep respect and gratitude. Rewilding, as an ethical orientation, invites us finally to mend the rift between ourselves and others. It lets us see and practice a way of being at home on Earth.

Cultivating care for others provides another essential ethical tool for living in the Anthropocene, namely a greater sensitivity to suffering. Today mitigation and adaptation represent the two main strategies for addressing climate change. Mitigation involves increasing energy efficiency, using solar and wind power, and otherwise working to reduce greenhouse gases. It seeks to stop climate change. Adaptation recognizes the limits of mitigation at this late date and, accepting some amount of warming, tries to protect people as much as possible from climate harm. Cities are building sea walls, utility companies are burying power lines, geneticists are developing drought resistant crops, and countries are devising evacuation plans in an attempt to blunt the most painful elements of climate change. Sadly, responding to climate change goes beyond these two approaches. No matter how much we mitigate or adapt to a warmer world, not everyone is able to dodge the climate bullet. Many people and certainly many other species are already suffering and will continue to suffer. As this intensifies, as people's lives are pulled out from under them, extending care to others and learning how to cope with increased pain will be essential capabilities. We need to develop individual and collective mechanisms for confronting the inevitability of climate suffering (Wapner 2014).

Rewilding involves turning off the impulse toward

mastery and opening up to greater unpredictability. As should be obvious, not everyone will embrace rewilding. Geoengineers, de-extinctionists, and others mesmerized by human ingenuity and technological wizardry will continue battling and trying to overtake global wildness. They are the heirs of modernist attempts to banish wildness, and we shouldn't expect them to abandon their vision of human betterment or cease from imposing human will on the planet as a whole. Nonetheless, while rewilding may be unable fully to dissuade those people whom Clive Hamilton (2013) calls "Earthmasters," it can still play a socially critical role by heightening moral reflection. Rewilding represents a voice of humility and of looking within. It casts a skeptical eye on the promise—and even value—of human control. While it may not silence the Promethean charge to impose human will on the planet, it can nonetheless badger moves toward mastery and therewith spawn greater moral reflection. It can, in other words, instill a dose of hesitation into the ranks of geoengineers and others. It can rankle the conscience and keep the question of human appropriateness alive.

Ethics may sound bland and inconsequential in the face of today's global emergencies. It may appear, especially in its guise of rewilding, as a strategy too soft and slow to respond to the feral, reeling world we live in. It may seem too humble for taking on, for instance, capitalism, state sovereignty, patriarchy, consumerism, and other political and economic structures that animate global wildness. But what is the alternative? People have been battling wildness for at least the past 10,000 years. They have much to show for it but, all along the way, there has been an itching suspicion that mastery may not be the primary attitude worthy of our humanity. Over the centuries, the powerful have enslaved fellow human beings, abused other creatures, and treated the Earth as a mere object to be exploited. This has produced wonders, but also great pain. Not only have others suffered, but the colonizers themselves have had to live with a moral blindness that has undermined the full expression of their humanity. Rewilding will not solve global environmental problems. It cannot guarantee physical well-being, or even survival. Nonetheless, it offers a key and necessary strategy. It advocates for greater climate mitigation, ecosystem preservation, and the humbling of human life so that other people and creatures and the living planet itself can thrive in concert with significant human presence. Moreover and perhaps more importantly, in addition to providing a reasonable strategic route into the future, it also affords a morally sensitive one. Climate change, biodiversity loss, freshwater scarcity, ozone depletion and other global environmental challenges are not puzzles in search of singular solutions; they are chronic challenges. They stand as the horizon for human life going forward. Rewilding attempts to address global problems concretelyand deepens our humanity. It offers a collectively new and necessary way of being human as we live through the portal of global environmental intensification.

*

The Earth is awash in wildness. For millennia, humans have pushed it to the margins. Their very success has eradicated it from some people's immediate lives but, as a result, thrown it into the lives of others and, importantly, onto the planet as a whole. The Earth is in spasm. We now face the task of either shoving wildness from the planet itself or befriending it. Neither promises salvation. One, however, offers not just a fighting chance but an end to fighting, and therewith an opportunity to enhance our ethical lives.

Wildness is not over. Long live the wild.

Further Reading

I have written this book with the general reader in mind. I have tried to avoid jargon and nitpicky scholarly debates in order to maintain a focus on what the fate of wildness means in an era of acute environmental intensification. The following pages provide guidance for delving deeper into humanity's long attempt to banish wildness and into how to confront global ecological spasm. My aim is not to be comprehensive or necessarily up-to-date (since the literature on wildness and environmental protection grows every day). Rather this is a compendium of additional readings that offer what I take to be the most rewarding elaborations of the book's central theme.

Thinkers have long wrestled with the concept of wildness. A challenge in navigating the literature is that writers have used the term in various ways. To get a sense of the diversity of meanings, you might begin with multicontributor volumes such as Peter Kahn, Jr. and Patricia Hasbach, eds., *The Rediscovery of the Wild* (MIT 2013); Gaven Van Horn and John Hausdoerffer, eds., *Wildness: Relations of People and Place* (University of Chicago Press 2017); and Cass Adams, ed., *The Soul Unearthed Through Nature: Celebrating Wildness and Spiritual Renewal* (Sentient 2002), which offer a variety of orientations. Wildness, in environmental literature, is usually associated with wilderness. Classic treatments include Henry David Thoreau, "Walking," *Atlantic Monthly* (June 1862); John Muir, *Our National Parks* (Houghton Mifflin 1901); and Aldo Leopold, *A Sand County Almanac and Sketches Here and There* (Oxford University Press 1949). For a historical overview of various understandings of wilderness, with a sensitivity to the concept of wildness, see J. Baird Callicott and Michael P. Nelson, eds., *The Great New Wilderness Debate* (University of Georgia Press 1998); Max Oelschlaeger, *The Idea of Wilderness: Prehistory to the Age of Ecology* (Yale University Press 1991); and Roderick Nash, *Wilderness and the American Mind* (Yale University Press 1969). William Cronon's two essays in his edited book, *Uncommon Ground: Rethinking the Human Place in Nature*

(Norton 1995), offer a wonderful way to appreciate the complex meanings of wilderness.

The question of wildness ending arises mostly from the humanization of the natural world. Bill McKibben's *The End of Nature* (Anchor 1989) initiated widespread reflection on how humans have interpenetrated the natural world, especially through climate change, and remains a powerful statement about the extent of humanity's presence on Earth. Geoscientists have given geological context to humanity's ubiquitous presence through the concept of the "Anthropocene." Paul Crutzen coined the term and first published about the concept in Paul Crutzen and Eugene Stoermer (2000), "The Anthropocene," *Global Change News*, 41: 17–18. Since then thinkers have reflected on the meaning of the Anthropocene for almost every academic discipline and aspect of life. One of the most penetrating and wide-ranging treatments is Clive Hamilton's *Defiant Earth: The Fate of Humans in the Anthropocene* (Polity 2017). In fact, after writing most of my book, I happened upon Hamilton's work and found common ground between his notion of the Earth as an "awakened giant" and my own notion of "brave new wildness." For a helpful guide to understanding the challenges of governance in a humanized world, see Frank Biermann,

Earth Systems Governance: World Politics in the Anthropocene (MIT 2014).

In chapter 2 I present a streamlined narrative of how humans came to see wildness as an enemy. The story, from the agricultural revolution through the modern period, is much more complex than I suggest. The factors shaping humanity's relationship with unpredictability go beyond economic, cultural, and political dimensions. To gain a more nuanced account, one can read about the interplay between capitalism and control over nature and other people in Jason Moore's monumental *Capitalism in the Web of Life: Ecology and the Accumulation of Capital* (Verso 2015). To appreciate the relationship between cultural norms, economic instrumentality, and the personal desire for control, see Elizabeth Shove, *Comfort, Cleanliness and Convenience: The Social Organization of Normality* (Berg 2003). Carolyn Merchant wrote a foundational text, explaining the influence of modern science, patriarchy, and the control of nature in *The Death of Nature: Women, Ecology, and the Scientific Revolution* (Harper 1982). Both Vandana Shiva, in *Staying Alive: Women, Ecology, and Development* (South End Press 1988), and Charlene Spretnak, in *The Resurgence of the Real: Body, Nature and Place in a Hypermodern World* (Addison-Wesley

1997), add depth to Merchant's insights and explain the intensification of control in modernity through feminist lenses. Readers can delve deeper into how humans first demonized wildness through various accounts of the agricultural revolution. My account rests mainly on two key texts: Roderick Nash, *Wilderness and the American Mind* (Yale University Press 1969)—which discusses how the shift from hunter-gatherers to agriculturalists involved gaining more control over nature and encouraged seeing the untamed world as wild—and James Scott, *Against the Grain: A Deep History of the Earliest States* (Yale University Press 2017)—which explains how elites manufactured agricultural sedentarism as a form of social control rather than as a promise of security and comfort.

Chapter 3 discusses how fossil fuels drove the industrial revolution and provided the means for significantly greater security and comfort. It also explains how this led to the global wilding of climate change. The literature on fossil fuel development is enormous. Many consider Daniel Yergin's *The Prize: The Epic Quest for Oil, Money, and Power* (Free Press 2008) a foundational historical account of oil. Aside from tracing oil since it was first discovered, this book emphasizes how oil has been used geostrategically by states to shape political affairs. More concrete and critical treatments of the politics of fossil fuels include Andreas Malm, *Fossil Capital: The Rise of Steam-Power and the Roots of Global Warming* (Verso 2015) and Timothy Mitchell, *Carbon Democracy: Political Power in the Age of Oil* (Verso 2013). These two highly insightful and sophisticated texts offer sensitive views on how oil, gas, and coal have been used as tools for power accumulation and projection. The literature on climate change is equally enormous. For powerful general treatments, see David Wallace-Wells, *The Uninhabitable Earth: Life After Warming* (Tim Duggan Books 2019), Bill McKibben, *Falter: Has the Human Game Begun to Play Itself Out?* (Henry Holt 2019), and Naomi Klein, *This Changes Everything: Capitalism Vs. the Climate* (Simon and Schuster 2015).

Chapter 3 ends by describing how geoengineers wish to extend control to the atmosphere itself as a response to climate change. The *Forum for Climate Engineering Assessment* (http://ceassessment.org) serves as a clearinghouse for scholarly and policy-related descriptions and evaluations of various geoengineering schemes and offers useful resources for learning about geoengineering in general. For an introduction to solar radiation management, see Jesse Reynolds, *The Governance of Solar*

Geoengineering: Managing Climate Change in the Anthropocene (Cambridge University Press 2019) and David Keith, *The Case for Climate Engineering* (MIT 2013). On carbon capture and sequestration, see Howard Herzog, *Carbon Capture* (MIT 2018); on carbon removal, see National Academies of Sciences et al., *Negative Emissions Technologies and Reliable Sequestration: A Research Agenda* (National Academies Press 2019).

Chapter 4 focuses on how beating out wildness leads to biodiversity loss and planetary endangerment. For general treatments of biodiversity loss, see, E. O. Wilson, *Half-Earth: Our Planet's Fight for Life* (Liveright 2017), Elizabeth Kolbert, *The Sixth Extinction: An Unnatural History* (Picador 2015) and Stephen Meyer, *The End of the Wild* (MIT 2006). Many factors now drive mass extinction. Among them is anthropocentrism and an ethical blindness to the plight of nonhuman creatures. The classic statement about anthropocentrism is Lynn White (1967), "The Historical Roots of the Environmental Crisis," *Science* 155 (3767): 1203–7. The foundational text on animal well-being is, Peter Singer, *Animal Liberation: A New Ethics for Our Treatment of Animals* (HarperCollins 1975). Many thinkers have been responsible for expanding ethics beyond humans, not only to animals but also to plants and nonliving features. Arne Naess was a vital figure in this movement of expansion, and his work has proved influential. For a useful overview of his orientation and of the movement it spawned, see Alan Drengson and Yuichi Inoue, eds., *The Deep Ecology Movement: An Introductory Anthology* (North Atlantic Books 1995). David Abram offers two powerful narratives in defense of ecocentric ethics: *The Spell of the Sensuous: Perception and Language in a More-than-Human World* (Vintage 1996) and *Becoming Animal: An Earthly Cosmology* (Vintage 2010). In *Braiding Sweetgrass: Indigenous Wisdom, Scientific Knowledge, and the Teachings of Plants* (Milkweed 2015), Robin Kimmermer demonstrates a sensitive appreciation for the subjectivity of plants and launches a moral invitation for us to live in reciprocal relationship with nature. Roger Gottlieb provides a comprehensive and extraordinarily readable guide to environmental ethics in *Morality and the Environmental Crisis* (Cambridge University Press 2019).

In response to global biodiversity loss, some thinkers recommend de-extinction. For an overview with sensitive reflection on the ethics of de-extinction, see Ben Minter, *The Fall of the Wild: Extinction, De-Extinction, and the Ethics of*

Conservation (Columbia University Press 2018), and Beth Shapiro, *How to Clone a Mammoth: The Science of De-Extinction* (Princeton University Press 2015). The strongest advocates of de-extinction are those associated with a Promethean orientation to environmentalism. Two environmental institutes of a Promethean character that focus on de-extinction are Revive & Restore (https://reviverestore.org) and the Breakthrough Institute (https://thebreak through.org).

Chapter 5 makes the case for rewilding in response to brave new wildness. For an overview of how the term is used, see Mihnea Tanasescu (2017), "Field Notes on the Meaning of Rewilding," *Ethics, Policy & Environment*, 20 (3): 333–49. Conservation biologists understand rewilding as an on-the-ground strategy of ecological protection. The classic text on this is Dave Foreman, *Rewilding North America: A Vision for Conservation in the 21st Century* (Island Press 2004). A more recent overview, primarily from a conservation perspective, is Nathalie Pettorelli, Sarah Durant and Johan T. du Toit, eds., *Rewilding* (Cambridge University Press 2019). Rewilding has relevance beyond conservation biology. George Monbiot offers a provocative general orientation in *Feral: Rewilding the Land, Sea, and Human Life* (University of Chicago 2017). Mark

Further Reading

Bekoff links conservation rewilding efforts with psychological and social dimensions in *Rewilding Our Hearts: Building Pathways of Compassion and Co-Existence* (New World Library 2014).

Part of rewilding, as I discuss it, involves appreciating the violence and ecological harm of racism, sexism, and classism and the othering of fellow humans and nature (what I call the "horizontal" dimension of wildness displacement) and building a more humane culture. Much of this is captured in the environmental justice literature, which is vast and growing. For a useful contemporary treatment of race, see Ghasson Hage, *Is Racism an Environmental Threat?* (Polity 2017); and, for a classic statement on race and environment, see Robert Bullard, *Dumping in Dixie: Race, Class, and Environmental Quality* (Westview 1990). On sexism and environment, see Greta Gaard's theoretically sophisticated study *Critical Ecofeminism* (Lexington 2019) and Nicole Detraz, *Gender and the Environment* (Polity 2016). Although not focused on environmental issues and wildness, one of the best treatments of 'otherness' and of the need to cultivate greater compassion for diverse ways of living is Andrew Solomon's *Far from the Tree: Parents, Children and the Search for Identity* (Scribner 2013). For a superb explication of how the lives of the privileged hold consequences for the poor and politically weak, see Rob Nixon, *Slow Violence and the Environmentalism of the Poor* (Harvard University Press 2013).

The concluding chapter argues for an ethical response to global wildness. While many worry about whether humanity will "make it," the chapter shifts the conversation to *how* humans will treat one another and the more-than-human world, as humanity lives through the opening portal of global spasm in the form of climate change, biodiversity loss, freshwater scarcity, deforestation, and so forth. It implicitly draws on the work of Dark Mountain, a collective of writers and other creatives who soberly try to weave broader meanings into this time of global ecological dismemberment, disruption, and planetary uncertainty. One of the best entryways into this perspective is Paul Kingsnorth, *Confessions of a Recovering Environmentalist and Other Essays* (Graywolf Press 2017). For a diverse set of Dark Mountain voices, see Dark Mountain Project, *Walking on Lava: Selected Works for Uncivilized Times* (Chelsea Green 2017). For a discussion of ethical responses from a more academic perspective, see Paul Wapner and Hilal Elver, eds., *Reimagining Climate Change* (Routledge 2017). Robert Bringhurst and Jan Zwicky offer a moving reflection on ethics in these critical times, in *Learning to Die: Wisdom in the Age of Climate Crisis* (University of Regina Press 2018). Finally, David Abram provides superb philosophical justifications for wild ethics in *The Spell of the Sensuous: Perception and Language in a More-than-Human World* (Vintage 1996) and *Becoming Animal: An Earthly Cosmology* (Vintage 2010).

References

Abram, D., 2012. *The spell of the sensuous: Perception and language in a more-than-human world*. New York: Vintage.

Abram, D., 2011. *Becoming animal*. New York: Vintage.

Agyeman, J., 2005. *Sustainable communities and the challenge of environmental justice*. New York: NYU Press.

Arendt, H., 1998. *The human condition*, 2nd edn. Chicago, IL: University of Chicago Press.

Assadourian, E., 2013. Re-engineering cultures to create a sustainable civilization. In Worldwatch Institute (ed.), *State of the World 2013*. Washington, DC: Island Press, pp. 113–25.

Beck, U., 1992. *Risk society: Towards a new modernity*. Thousand Oaks, CA: SAGE.

Bekoff, M., 2014. *Rewilding our hearts: Building pathways of compassion and coexistence*. Novato, CA: New World Library.

References

Bernstein, P. L., 1996. *Against the gods: The remarkable story of risk*. New York: John Wiley & Sons.

Bringhurst, R., and Zwicky, J., 2018. *Learning to die: Wisdom in the age of climate crisis*. Regina, Canada: University of Regina Press.

Bullard, R. D., 2000. *Dumping in Dixie: Race, class, and environmental quality*. New York: Routledge.

Cox, S., and Cox, P., 2016. *How the world breaks: Life in catastrophe's path, from the Caribbean to Siberia*. New York: New Press.

Daily CO_2, 2019. Daily CO_2. CO2.Earth, NOAA. https://www.co2.earth/daily-co2.

Detraz, N., 2017. *Gender and the environment*. Hoboken, NJ: John Wiley & Sons Ltd.

Eule, S., 2019. International energy agency releases its world energy outlook. Global Energy Institute. https://www.globalenergyinstitute.org/international-energy-agency-releases-its-world-energy-outlook.

Flannery, T., 2017. Tim Flannery speculates that whole extinct species could be resurrected, Financial Review, April 27, https://www.afr.com/technology/mike-flannery-speculates-that-whole-extinct-species-could-be-resurrected-20170409-gvgxwo.

Foreman, D., 2004. *Rewilding North America: A vision for conservation in the 21st century*. Washington, DC: Island Press.

Frame, D., Joshi, M., Hawkins, E., Harrington, L., and de Roiste, M., 2017. Population-based emergence of unfamiliar climates. *Nature Climate Change*, 7: 407–11.

Gardiner, S. M., 2011. *A perfect moral storm: The ethical tragedy of climate change*. Oxford: Oxford University Press.

Gorvett, Z., 2016. How a giant space umbrella could stop global warming. BBC.com. http://www.bbc.com/future/story/20160425-how-a-giant-space-umbrella-could-stop-global-warming.

Griffin, P., 2017. CDP Carbon Majors Report 2017. Carbon Disclosure Project (CDP). https://b8f65cb37 3b1b7b15feb-c70d8ead6ced550b4d987d7c03fcdd1d .ssl.cf3.rackcdn.com/cms/reports/documents/000/002/327/original/Carbon-Majors-Report-2017.pdf.

Hage, G., 2017. *Is racism an environmental threat?* Hoboken, NJ: John Wiley & Sons, Inc.

Hall, S., 2015. Exxon knew about climate change almost 40 years ago. *Scientific American*, 26. https://www.scientificamerican.com/article/exxon-knew-about-climate-change-almost-40-years-ago.

Hamilton, C., 2013. *Earthmasters: The dawn of the age of climate engineering*. New Haven, CT: Yale University Press.

Hamilton, C., 2017. *Defiant earth: The fate of humans in the Anthropocene*. Cambridge: Polity.

Heath, J. M., 2017. *Warfare in Neolithic Europe: An archaeological and anthropological analysis*. Barnsley, UK: Pen and Sword.

References

Herzog, H., 2018. *Carbon Capture*. Cambridge, MA: MIT Press.

Jones, A., Haywood, J. M., Alterskjær, K., Boucher, O., Cole, J. N., Curry, C. L., Irvine, P. J., Ji, D., Kravitz, B., and Kristjánsson, J. E., 2013. The impact of abrupt suspension of solar radiation management (termination effect) in experiment G2 of the Geoengineering Model Intercomparison Project (GeoMIP). *Journal of Geophysical Research: Atmospheres*, 118: 9743–52.

Jones, N., 2017. How the world passed a carbon threshold and why it matters. *Yale Environment 360*, January 26. https://e360.yale.edu/features/how-the-world-passed-a-carbon-threshold-400ppm-and-why-it-matters.

Kimmerer, R. W., 2013. *Braiding sweetgrass: Indigenous wisdom, scientific knowledge and the teachings of plants*. Minneapolis, MN: Milkweed Editions.

Klein, N., 2014. *This changes everything*. New York: Simon & Schuster.

Klepeis, N. E., Nelson, W. C., Ott, W. R., Robinson, J. P., Tsang, A. M., Switzer, P., Behar, J. V., Hern, S. C., and Engelmann, W. H., 2001. The National Human Activity Pattern Survey (NHAPS): A resource for assessing exposure to environmental pollutants. *Journal of Exposure Science & Environmental Epidemiology*, 11: 231–52.

Kolbert, E., 2014. *The sixth extinction: An unnatural history*. New York: Henry Holt.

References

Leopold, A., 1989. *A Sand County almanac, and sketches here and there*. New York: Oxford University Press.

Lerner, S., 2010. *Sacrifice zones: The front lines of toxic chemical exposure in the United States*. Cambridge, MA: MIT Press.

Macnaghten, P., and Szerszynski, B., 2013. Living the global social experiment: An analysis of public discourse on solar radiation management and its implications for governance. *Global Environmental Change*, 23: 465–74.

Malm, A., 2016. *Fossil capital: The rise of steam power and the roots of global warming*. London: Verso.

Mann, C., 2014. State of the species. In S. Nicholson, and P. Wapner (eds.), *Global environmental politics: From person to planet*. Abingdon: Routledge, pp. 17–23.

Mann, C., 2018. *The wizard and the prophet: Two remarkable scientists and their dueling visions to shape tomorrow's world*. New York: Knopf.

McKibben, B., 2012. Global warming's terrifying new math. *Rolling Stone*, August 2, 2012. https://www.rollingstone.com/author/bill-mckibben.

McKibben, B., 2019. *Falter: Has the human game begun to play itself out?* New York: Henry Holt.

Merchant, C., 1990. *The death of nature: Women, ecology, and the scientific revolution*. New York: Harper One.

Meyer, S., 2006. *The end of the wild*. Cambridge, MA: MIT Press.

References

Minteer, B.A., 2018. *The fall of the wild: Extinction, de-extinction, and the ethics of conservation*. New York: Columbia University Press.

Mitchell, T., 2011. *Carbon democracy: Political power in the age of oil*. London: Verso.

Monbiot, G., 2015. *Feral: Rewilding the land, the sea, and human life*. Chicago, IL: University of Chicago Press.

Moore, J. W., 2015. *Capitalism in the web of life: Ecology and the accumulation of capital*. London: Verso.

Moreno-Cruz, J. B., Ricke, K. L., and Keith, D. W., 2012. A simple model to account for regional inequalities in the effectiveness of solar radiation management. *Climatic Change*, 110 (3–4): 649–68.

Mueller, M. L., 2017. *Being salmon, being human: Encountering the wild in us and us in the wild*. White River Junction, VT: Chelsea Green Publishing.

Muir, J., 2011. *Wilderness essays*. Layton, UT: Gibbs Smith.

Naess, A., 1973. The shallow and the deep, long-range ecology movement: A summary. *Inquiry*, 16: 95–100.

Nash, R., 2014. *Wilderness and the American mind*. Yale, CT: Yale University Press.

National Academies of Sciences, Engineering, and Medicine, 2018. Direct air capture and mineral carbonation approaches for carbon dioxide removal and reliable sequestration. In *Proceedings of a workshop: In brief*. Washington, DC: National Academies Press. https://www.nap.edu/read/25132/chapter/1#10.

Nixon, R., 2011. *Slow violence and the environmentalism of the poor*. Cambridge, MA: Harvard University Press.

O'Connor, M. R., 2015. *Resurrection science: Conservation, de-extinction and the precarious future of wild things*. New York: St. Martins Press.

Oreskes, N., and Conway, E. M., 2011. *Merchants of doubt: How a handful of scientists obscured the truth on issues from tobacco smoke to global warming*. New York: Bloomsbury.

Pollan, M., 2013. The intelligent plant. *New Yorker*, December 15. https://www.newyorker.com/magazine/2013/12/23/the-intelligent-plant.

Regan, T., 2004. *The case for animal rights*. Berkeley: University of California Press.

Rochon, E., 2008. *False hope why carbon capture and storage won't save the climate*. Greenpeace International. http://www.precaution.org/lib/gp_report_false_hope.080505.pdf.

Scott, J. C., 2017. *Against the grain: A deep history of the earliest states*. New Haven, CT: Yale University Press.

Shapiro, B., 2015. *How to clone a mammoth: The science of de-extinction*. Princeton, NJ: Princeton University Press.

References

Shove, E., 2003. *Comfort, cleanliness and convenience.* Oxford: Berg.

Spretnak, C., 2012. *The resurgence of the real: Body, nature and place in a hypermodern world.* New York: Routledge.

Tanasescu, M., 2017. Field Notes on the Meaning of Rewilding. *Ethics, Policy & Environment,* 20: 333–49.

Taylor, D., 2014. *Toxic communities: Environmental racism, industrial pollution, and residential mobility.* New York: NYU Press.

Thoreau, H. D., 1992. *Walden and other writings,* B. Atkitson (ed.). New York: Random House.

UNFCCC, 1992. *United Nations framework on climate change: Article 2.* https://unfccc.int/resource/docs/convkp/conveng.pdf.

Use it and lose it: The outsize effect of US consumption on the environment. 2002. *Scientific American,* September 14. https://www.scientificamerican.com/article/american-consumption-habits.

Wallace-Wells, D., 2019. *The uninhabitable earth: Life after warming.* New York: Tim Duggan Books.

Wapner, P., 2014. Climate suffering. *Global Environmental Politics,* 14 (2): 1–6.

White, L., 1967. The historical roots of our ecologic crisis. *Science,* 155: 1203–7.

Willow, A. J., 2018. *Understanding extrACTIVISM: Culture and power in nature resource disputes.* New York: Routledge.

References

Wohlleben, P., 2016. *The hidden life of trees: What they feel, how they communicate: Discoveries from a secret world*. Vancouver, BC: Greystone Books.

World Bank Group, 2019. CO2 emissions (kt). *World Bank Data Journal Online*. https://data.worldbank.org/indicator/EN.ATM.CO2E.KT?view=map.

Zachos, E., March 30, 2018. 2,400 animals die in oil spill in Colombia. *National Geographic*. https://news.nationalgeographic.com/2018/03/oil-spill-colombia-animals-killed-spd.